A COMMENTARY ON TENNYSON'S
IN MEMORIAM

A

Commentary on
Tennyson's
In Memoriam

By
A. C. Bradley
Formerly Professor of Poetry in the University of Oxford

Third Edition, Revised

ARCHON BOOKS

HAMDEN, CONNECTICUT

1966

TO
THE BELOVED MEMORY
OF
GEORGE GROVE

PREFACE TO THE THIRD EDITION.

In the interest of possessors of the Second
Edition, it has seemed best to leave the Commentary unchanged (save for the removal of two
or three misprints), and to place the additions and
corrections which distinguish this Edition in an
Appendix by themselves.

They are occasioned, for the most part, by the
appearance of the present Lord Tennyson's edition
of *In Memoriam* (1905), which contains, together
with matter already used in the preparation of this
Commentary, a number of notes written or dic-
tated by the poet himself, and others contributed
by the editor. The former are referred to in my
Appendix as 'the Author's notes.' Generally,
they must be taken as decisive, though it should
be borne in mind that, as was natural, the poet in
his later years did not in all cases remember his
original meaning accurately (see *e.g.* the note on

'the sea-blue bird of March' on p. 186 of the Commentary).

With one or two exceptions, I have referred only to such notes in Lord Tennyson's edition as confirm, correct, or illustrate my own interpretations.   There are many other interesting notes, which the reader should consult.

April, 1910.

PREFACE TO THE ISSUE OF 1915.

SEE two additional notes on p. 251.

May, 1915.

PREFACE TO THE FIRST EDITION.

As most readers of a book are said to ignore the Preface, I will beg anyone who may intend to use this Commentary to read, for his own sake, the first two of the following paragraphs.

The stanzas beginning *Strong Son of God*, with which *In Memoriam* opens, are called in these pages the 'Prologue'; the stanzas at the end, beginning *O true and tried*, the 'Epilogue'; the 131 intervening pieces are called 'sections,' or, where the word could not be misunderstood, 'poems.' The sections are referred to by Roman numerals, their lines by Arabic: thus 'XL. 10' means 'section XL., line 10.' I found it indispensable to refer usually to lines, not stanzas. In the case of the shorter sections this will give the reader no trouble, but he will find it convenient to number the lines of a few longer ones. I am sorry that in referring to many of Tennyson's other poems I was unable to guide the reader to the passage in question, as the lines are not numbered.

The text used is of course the copyright text, which has remained unaltered, I believe, since 1884. The changes made up to that time are noted where they occur, and are also printed in a list at the end of the book. Two of them are important. In the fourth edition, 1851, section LIX., *O Sorrow, wilt thou live with me*, appeared for the first time. In 1870 section XXXIX., *Old warder of these buried bones*, was added. Readers who use one of the first three editions, or again an edition later than the third and earlier than 1872, must modify my references accordingly; but they will find it simpler to buy the present text for sixpence.

The purpose of this book is strictly limited. My main object is to be of use to such readers as care to study *In Memoriam* closely, by showing the bearing of the sections on one another, and by dealing with many of the difficulties of interpretation which I have encountered in my own reading of the poem, in conversation, in teaching,[1] and in books on the subject. The quotations of parallel passages are sometimes meant to serve this latter purpose, sometimes merely to gratify literary

[1] The book had its origin in lectures given in 1884 at University College, Liverpool.

curiosity regarding the point discussed at the end of the Introduction. I have abstained almost wholly from 'aesthetic criticism,' chiefly because, although of course it interests me more than the kind of comment to which this book is restricted, I do not think the two kinds harmonise well.

I ought perhaps to say a few words to those readers who, without objecting on principle to all commentaries on English poetry, may naturally feel doubts about this particular book.

To those who think all commentary on *In Memoriam* superfluous, I will venture to reply that they can never have studied the poem. If they do so they will certainly find that the meaning of many passages is doubtful, and that a few are extremely obscure ; the cause of these defects being sometimes excess in the Tennysonian virtue of conciseness, sometimes an excessive or unfortunate use of periphrasis or decoration.

Others will think that, at any rate, many lines which I have annotated are quite perspicuous. I agree with them ; but I believe I have attempted to explain nothing that I had not found misunderstood by myself or someone else ; and there are hosts of misapprehensions which I have left unnoticed. The exasperated reader should try the experiment of questioning himself and a few other intelligent persons on the meaning of every line in a dozen sections taken at hap-hazard from the poem.

I have more difficulty in meeting the possible charge that I often insist on finding a definite meaning where there is none ; for this charge raises a question too wide to discuss in a Preface. I can only say that, while I have no doubt it may be true as regards some passages, I question the presupposition on which it rests. Apart from defects, fine poetry, I think, is indefinite, in the sense that its language has a vague suggestiveness, on which its virtue largely depends and which disappears in a paraphrase. But this suggestiveness, or untranslateable 'meaning,' attaches to a definite mental matter, namely images and thoughts, the outlines of which should be clear to us, however little we may be able to exhaust their significance. We read for the most part half-asleep, but a poet writes wide-awake. His thoughts may be unlike logical statements, and his images may conflict, but they are there and all alive ; and our business is to recreate them. We are much mistaken when we foist upon him the misty generalities which his words may at first convey to us. There is no poetry in *this* indefiniteness, there is simply feebleness of imagination.

Lastly, I may be told that in any case it is idle to trouble oneself about those puzzles whose solution would bring hardly any poetical profit, and absurd to write pages on 'God shut the doorways of his head.' Perhaps. But, to go no further, there are people who cannot be content to live with such puzzles in a poem that they love. I shall be satisfied if my book helps them to read *In Memoriam* without a check, or saves them from spending on its difficulties one hundredth part of the labour I have spent.

I am under obligations to the following among books which I have consulted: Lord Tennyson's *Memoir* of his father, first edition, in two volumes; Mr. Churton Collins's *Illustrations of Tennyson*; Dr. Gatty's *Key to In Memoriam*, fourth edition; Mr. J. F. Genung's *Tennyson's In Memoriam*: *its Purpose and its Structure*; Miss E. R. Chapman's *Companion to In Memoriam*; Mr. E. C. Tainsh's *Study of Tennyson's Works*, new edition, 1893; Mr. James Knowles's article in *The Nineteenth Century* for January, 1893. Where I was conscious of a particular obligation I have specially acknowledged it, but I may not always have remembered my debts, and I should like to say that, though I differ from him constantly, I think Mr. Genung's book has not met with full recognition.

I am greatly obliged to Mr. C. E. Benham, of Colchester, who lent me the manuscript of his able paraphrase of the poem. Some of his interpretations are quoted in my notes.

My friend Mr. Beeching's edition of *In Memoriam* was not published till my work was practically complete and partly in type. His name is mentioned where I have made changes or additions after reading his book, but I may have left references to 'the commentators' which do not apply to him.

Finally, I owe thanks to my friends Messrs. MacLehose for the care with which they have printed a troublesome manuscript, and to many other friends for help given to me in preparing the Commentary ; not least to my brother-in-law, the late Sir George Grove, who brought to the study of the poem that enthusiasm and genius in appreciation, to which so many thousands of lovers of music are indebted. Among several reasons why I regret a long delay in the publication of my book the chief is that he cannot see the pages to which he would have given so eager a welcome.

LONDON, *May*, 1901.

PREFACE TO THE SECOND EDITION.

FOR this edition not many changes have been made in the Introduction, but a great many in the Commentary. Notes or parts of notes on a few lines have been omitted as needless. I have added explanations of other passages which I had supposed to require none. And in the notes on some of the specially troublesome lines I have made alterations or additions, either to support my opinion, or to show why I have changed it, or to mention interpretations which, without having convinced me, seem to me not improbable. Where the new matter takes the form of a note on the old it is often printed within square brackets. For the convenience of owners of the first edition I give a list of the passages where important changes have been made in the Commentary, without noticing the minor improvements which occur on almost every page: II. 11, 12; III. 6,

10; XIII. 1-4; XXIV. 15, 16; XXXIX. 8-12;
XLIII. 11, 12; XLIV. 4; XLV. 9; XLVI.; LVI. 28;
LXXXI; LXXXV. 101; LXXXVI. 13-16; XCII. 13;
XCIII. 5-8; XCV. 36, 37; XCVI. 22 ff.; XCIX. 9;
CXVIII. 16; CXIX. 4; CXXII.; CXXV. 2.

For a good many of the alterations so far mentioned I am indebted, wholly or in part, to others.
I have consulted Mr. Robinson's edition of the
poem, and Mr. Jacobs's *Tennyson and In Memoriam.* Mr. H. W. Eve and Mr. Walter Larden
sent me valuable suggestions. Two reviews of
my first edition have been of use to me in preparing the second, that of Professor Beeching in
the *Guardian* of September 11, 1901, and that of
Mr. Cecil Nolan Ferrall in the *Weekly Register* of
November 29, 1901; and Mr. Ferrall has also
most kindly helped me by giving me his opinion
on a number of doubtful passages. These obligations are acknowledged in detail in the notes.
Finally, I owe thanks not least to the comments
of several relatives and friends.

In addition to these changes I have considerably increased the number of references to parallel
passages. And here I have to thank for their
help several correspondents, including some of
the persons already mentioned, and especially the
Bishop of Derry, who lent me his copy of *In*

Memoriam, in which a very large number of interesting parallels are noted. Those which I have used are marked with his initials (G.A.C.), and I should have liked to quote a great many more, but I have thought it best to abide by the rule of giving only such passages as I thought might not improbably have influenced Tennyson. I must add that my insertion of a parallel does not necessarily mean that I think there *was* such influence; and the question whether there was or not has, for me, merely a biographical or psychological interest. It appears to me as absurd to fancy that Tennyson's mastery of phrase is called in question by his reminiscences of other men's phrases as to suppose that Milton's mastery is impugned by the delightful collection of parallels in Warton's edition of the Minor Poems.

In the Preface to the first edition I mentioned, out of a regard for University College, Liverpool, that this book had its origin in lectures given there in 1884. I am anxious to guard against a misapprehension to which this statement has given rise. My book, in much that it contains and much that it omits, is very different from those lectures, and it is far from representing the kind of matter which, in my judgment, a teacher of English

Literature should offer to his students. To abstain almost wholly from literary discussion of a poem, and to dwell at length upon its most obscure passages, would be, I should say, the very way *not* to 'teach literature.'

June, 1902.

CONTENTS

INTRODUCTION

I.

THE ORIGIN OF *IN MEMORIAM.*

'IT must be remembered,' writes Tennyson in a note on *In Memoriam*, 'that this is a poem, *not* an actual biography. . . . The different moods of sorrow as in a drama are dramatically given, and my conviction that fear, doubts, and suffering will find answer and relief only through Faith in a God of Love. "I" is not always the author speaking of himself, but the voice of the human race speaking through him.'[1]

This being so, it would seem that, in order to understand the poem, we need know nothing of the circumstances which occasioned it, any more than we require a knowledge of the lives of Shakespeare or of Gray in order to understand *Hamlet* or the *Elegy*. But *In Memoriam* is not

[1] *Memoir*, I, p. 305.

A

quite like *Hamlet* or Gray's *Elegy*; it rather resembles such a poem as *Adonais*. Just as *Adonais* contains allusions which would not be fully intelligible to a reader ignorant of the literary history of the time, so *In Memoriam* contains references which can be understood but imperfectly from the poem itself; and as in this case the persons and events referred to belong chiefly to private life, the reader cannot be assumed to have any knowledge of them at all. It is desirable, accordingly, to summarize the necessary information at once, and in the notes on particular sections or passages the reader will be asked to turn for explanation to this summary. To it will be added a few remarks on Arthur Hallam's character and writings.

The poem was written ' In Memoriam A. H. H. Obiit MDCCCXXXIII.' A. H. H. was Arthur Henry Hallam, son of Henry Hallam the historian. He was born on February 1st, 1811, and was thus about eighteen months younger than Tennyson (born August 6th, 1809). They formed, at Trinity College, Cambridge, an intimate friendship which lasted nearly five years. They travelled together on the Rhine and in France. Hallam visited Tennyson's home, and became engaged to the poet's sister Emily. After leaving

Cambridge he began to read for the bar, living in his father's house in London (67 Wimpole Street). In the summer of 1833 he made a tour on the Continent with his father; and at Vienna, on September 15th, died very suddenly and unexpectedly of a stroke of apoplexy. His body was brought by sea from Trieste to England, and was buried at Clevedon, on the Bristol Channel, on January 3rd, 1834; Clevedon Court being the residence of Sir Abraham Elton, Baronet, Hallam's grandfather on the mother's side.

The poem contains references to many of these facts, and also to some matters not directly connected with Arthur Hallam. Thus the marriage tour, in 1836, of the poet's brother Charles was the occasion of section XCVIII. Edmund Lushington, who became Professor of Greek at Glasgow, was the friend addressed in LXXXV., and the Epilogue celebrates his marriage with the poet's sister Cecilia in 1842. Tennyson's early home, the rectory of Somersby, half-way between Horncastle and Spilsby in Lincolnshire, is referred to in XXVIII.-XXX., LXXVIII., LXXXIX., XCV. The family left Somersby in 1837 (C.-CIII.), and settled at High Beech, Epping Forest (CIV.-CV.).

To describe a character in lyrical verse which scrupulously avoids prosaic expressions must be a most difficult task. Perhaps Tennyson felt this, for the sections of *In Memoriam* which attempt to fulfil it come late in the poem and seem to be introduced chiefly in order to portray certain characteristics of the ideal humanity of the future. Nor can they be said to convey a vivid idea of Arthur Hallam to those who never saw him. The chief impressions left by them are of a very unusual completeness of character, of an equally rare absence of defects, and of a promise which seemed to his friends almost boundless. But the image is vague, and there is some excuse for those who, judging merely from the poem, have suspected Tennyson of greatly over-estimating his friend. The suspicion makes little or no difference to their appreciation of *In Memoriam*, but it is probably groundless. The accounts of Arthur Hallam given by his other contemporaries closely resemble Tennyson's. Their estimate is the same; and to say that similar estimates may be found in any memoir of a promising youth who died prematurely is quite untrue. His college friends 'invariably agreed that it was of him above all his contemporaries that great and lofty expectations were to be formed.'[1] His school-fellows thought

[1] *Remains in Verse and Prose of Arthur Henry Hallam*, New Edition, 1863.

that it was rather he than Gladstone that was
to be the great man. His father, one whose
sobriety of judgment would not be overwhelmed
by affection or grief, described him as an 'extraordinary young man'; and the sentence, 'He
seemed to tread the earth as a spirit from some
better world,' does not sound exaggerated among
the testimonies of Hallam's friends. To the end
of his days Tennyson retained the opinion he had
formed in youth. Mr. Gladstone, in an extremely
interesting article written late in life,[1] spoke of
Hallam thus: 'Among his contemporaries at
Eton . . . he stood supreme . . . and the long
life through which I have since wound my way,
and which has brought me into contact with so
many men of rich endowments, leaves him where
he then stood so far as my estimation is concerned. . . . It is the simple truth that Arthur
Henry Hallam was a spirit so exceptional that
everything with which he was brought into relation . . . came to be, through this contact,
glorified by a touch of the ideal. . . . It is a
true case of *ostendent terris hunc tantum fata* : he
resembled a passing emanation from some other
and less darkly chequered world.' Such testimonies as these are irresistible, and they go far to

[1] It was published in *The Daily Telegraph* for January 5, 1898.

explain what has been criticised as the excessive
humility of some parts of *In Memoriam*.

One passage in Mr. Gladstone's article has a
special interest when placed side by side with the
section of *In Memoriam* which describes Hallam's
probable attitude towards the political movement
of the time (CXIII.). 'It is evident,' Mr. Gladstone writes, 'that the great and sudden augmenta-
tion of liberty in a thousand forms places under
an aggravated strain the balance which governs
humanity both in thought and conduct. And I
have never . . . known a man who seemed to me
to possess all the numerous and varied quali-
fications required in order to meet the growing
demand, and even its fullest breadth, in anything
like the measure in which Arthur Hallam exhi-
bited these budding, nay, already flowering gifts.'
But Tennyson writes of the dangers of political
progress, and Mr. Gladstone has in view those of
progress in thought. These are, indeed, alluded
to in *In Memoriam*, CXIV.: but while the poet
seems to have considered that Hallam's sphere
was likely to be that of public life, the statesman
looked to his fulfilling a similar function as a
writer on philosophy or theology.

Any estimate of the volume of *Remains* would
lead us too far from our purpose, but a few

passages in it are of immediate interest to readers
of Tennyson. Some phrases recall similar phrases
in his poems, though we cannot say whether the
similarity is due to coincidence, or to unconscious
reminiscence on the part of the poet, or even to
the use by Hallam of expressions caught from the
talk of his friend. Thus the lines (p. 56),

> My own dear sister, thy career
>   Is all before thee, *thorn and flower* ;

and the lines (p. 84),

> Still am I free to close my happy eyes,
>   And *paint upon the gloom* thy mimic form,

recall *In Memoriam*, XLVI. 2, and LXX. 2. When
we find Chaucer described as ' our beautiful morn-
ing-star' we remember the opening stanza of the
Dream of Fair Women.[1] The words, ' that indeed
is in the power of God's election, with whom
alone rest the *abysmal secrets of personality*' (p.
359), remind us of the words in *The Palace of
Art*,

> God, before whom ever lie bare
> The abysmal deeps of Personality.

Tennyson's references to the early history of

---

[1] I do not mean to imply that no one had used the phrase before.
It occurs, for instance, in Denham.

the earth are paralleled by the following lines to Ben Lomond (p. 12):

> Oh, if thy dread original were not sunk
> I' th' mystery of universal birth,
> What joy to know thy tale of mammoths huge,
> And formings rare of the material prime,
> And terrible craters, cold a cycle since![1]

Like the poet, too, Hallam seems to have had a strong feeling of the utter insignificance of the earth in the 'immense scheme' (p. 360).

As we know from the *Memoir*, Tennyson did not by any means fully share his friend's apprehensions about the political future, but some words of Hallam's (*Remains*, p. 144) might be taken as a commentary on *In Memoriam*, CXXVII.: ' Looking then to the lurid presages of the times that are coming; believing that amidst the awful commotions of society, which few of us do not expect— the disruption, it may be, of those common bonds which hold together our social existence, necessarily followed by an occurrence on a larger scale of the same things that were witnessed in France forty years ago. . . .'

The two friends must often have talked together of that belief in love as the central meaning of things which with Hallam was evidently partly

---

[1] 'Cycle' is common in Tennyson: 'material prime' occurs in *The Two Voices*.

due to his study of Plato, Dante, and Petrarch, and which took a curious shape in his *Theodicæa Novissima*; and such sentences as the following (and there are not a few of the kind) have much of the spirit of parts of *In Memoriam*: 'But it was not in scattered sonnets[1] that the whole magnificence of that idea could be manifested, which represents love as at once the base and the pyramidal point of the entire universe, and teaches us to regard the earthly union of souls, not as a thing accidental, transitory, and dependent on the condition of human society, but with far higher import, as the best and the appointed symbol of our relations with God, and through them of his own ineffable essence' (p. 130). This 'idea' is, in essentials, the same as 'that solemn idea which alone solves the enigma of our feelings, and while it supplies a meaning to conscience, explains the destination of man' (p. 170. The student of *In Memoriam* will find it worth while to read the whole passage down to p. 177).

I do not intend to imply by these remarks that, of the two friends, Hallam had the more original and influential mind. We have little evidence, and it is quite possible that many of the ideas in the *Remains* were not merely common to the two,

[1] He is referring to Dante.

but passed from Tennyson to Hallam. What
seems nearly certain is that Hallam was more
inclined to philosophical and theological speculation than his friend then was, and much more
inclined to formulate the results of such speculation than Tennyson ever became.

II.

THE COMPOSITION OF *IN MEMORIAM*.

WHEN was *In Memoriam* written? We know that its occasion was the death of Arthur Hallam in 1833, and that it was published first in 1850.[1] Do we know anything of the date of its composition beyond the fact that it came into being during those seventeen years?

In considering this question we must be on our guard against inferences drawn from what may be called the internal chronology of the poem. It will be shown presently that the author almost certainly intended to produce the impression that the 131 sections cover a period of about three years. But *In Memoriam* is 'a poem, *not* an actual biography.' The poet who speaks in its

[1] Without sections XXXIX. and LIX. of the present text. See notes on these.

various sections is not precisely the same person
as the author who composed and arranged them.
And if the latter thought it well to convey the
idea that the 'progress of sorrow' portrayed in his
work was complete within a certain time, this gives
us no ground for supposing that the like progress
in his own life was of the same duration, and still
less for imagining that the dates of the composition of the various sections correspond to the positions of those sections in the internal chronology
of three years.

Turning then to the evidence, we find the following indications :

(1) *Statements as to date by Tennyson himself.*

(*a*) The Prologue is dated 1849.

(*b*) The Epilogue (9, 10) contains a direct
statement which cannot refer to the internal
chronology.   After an allusion to the 'dark day'
of his friend's death the poet goes on,

> Tho' I since then have number'd o'er
> Some thrice three years.

This gives the date as about 1842, and this was
the year of the marriage of Edmund Lushington
with Cecilia Tennyson, which, the poet himself
says, was the occasion of his Epilogue.

(*c*) In a letter to Aubrey de Vere, Tennyson
writes : ' With respect to the " Elegies," I cannot

say that I have turned my attention to them lately. I do not know whether I have done anything new in that quarter since you saw them, but I believe I am going to print them' (*Memoir*, I. 282). The date is apparently 1848. His correspondent first met the poet in 1841 or 1842 (*ib.* 207), but there is nothing to show when he had last seen the " Elegies."

(*d*) In CXXVII. the phrase ' the red fool-fury of the Seine' does not refer to 1848, as it was ' probably written long before '48.' [1]

(*e*) Finally, the following sentences may be quoted from Tennyson's note on *In Memoriam* in the *Memoir* (I. 304, 305): ' The sections were written at many different places, and as the phases of our intercourse came to my memory and suggested them. I did not write them with any view of weaving them into a whole, or for publication, until I found that I had written so many.'

(2) *Statements as to date by the present Lord Tennyson.*

(*a*) In the *Memoir* we are told that the first-written sections of the poem were the following (I have inserted the numbers):

---

[1] Authoritative words in Gatty's *Key*, p. 138. I suppose they apply to the whole section.

Fair ship that from the Italian shore (IX).
With trembling fingers did we weave (XXX.)
When Lazarus left his charnel cave (XXXI.)
This truth came borne with bier and pall (LXXXV.)[1]
It draweth near the birth of Christ (XXVIII., now
    'The time draws near');

that the 'earliest jottings of the "Elegies" were begun in 1833'; and that the sections just named (which, I presume, are the earliest jottings') are found in a manuscript book containing also the earliest version of *The. Two Voices*, which 'was begun under the cloud of this overwhelming sorrow.'[2]

(*b*) It is also stated that 'the sections of *In Memoriam* about Evolution had been read by [Tennyson's] friends some years before the publication of the *Vestiges of Creation* in 1844' (*ib.* 223). Unfortunately the sections are not

---

[1] If the reader remembers that this is the retrospective section of thirty stanzas addressed to Edmund Lushington, he will be startled to learn its date. Certainly, if we had only internal evidence to rely on, a suggestion that this poem was written soon after Hallam's death would be considered almost absurd; see, for instance, lines 61 ff. It is difficult not to suspect that the section, as we have it, has been greatly changed; or even that the first stanza alone is early. Observe the break between that stanza and the second.

[2] *Memoir*, I. 109, 297; cf. 139. The likeness of some of the ideas and expressions in sections XLIII.-XLVII. and in *The Two Voices* may be significant.

specified; but LV., LVI., CXVIII., and CXXIII. are presumably among them.

(3) *Statements from which dates may be inferred*. Either from the *Memoir* or from authoritative insertions in Gatty's *Key* we gain the following results.

(*a*) Section XCVIII. refers to an event of 1836, the marriage-tour of Charles Tennyson and his bride.

(*b*) Sections C.-CIII. allude to the removal of the Tennysons from Somersby in 1837.

(*c*) Sections CIV.-V. allude to their new home at High Beech, Epping Forest.

(*d*) Section LXXXVI. was written at Barmouth, and Tennyson was at Barmouth in 1839, while the *Memoir* does not, I think, mention any previous visit to that place.[1]

(*e*) Edmund Lushington's notes, referring to Christmas 1841, contain the statement; 'the number of the memorial poems had rapidly increased since I had seen the poet, his book containing many that were new to me'; and he appears to have seen the poet last in the summer of 1840 (*Memoir*, I. 201, 202). He mentions VI.

---

[1] Nor have I found any reference in the *Memoir* before 1844 to a visit to Gloucestershire, which Tennyson mentions among the localities in which the poems were written (*Memoir*, I. 305).

as though it were one of these new poems, and he says that LI. was 'just composed.'

(*f*) Even after 1841 new sections seem to have been added, for Lushington says that in 1845 Tennyson 'showed [him] those poems of *In Memoriam* which were finished and which were a perfectly novel surprise to [him]';[1] and the words, 'he had then completed many of the cantos in *In Memoriam*,' would naturally imply that other cantos are later than 1845 (*ib.* 203).

(*g*) It would appear from Rawnsley's *Memories of the Tennysons*, page 121, that CXXI. was composed shortly before the publication of *In Memoriam*.

(4) *Indications in the poem.* A few passages seem not quite consistent with the internal chronology, and these may point to a comparatively late date of composition. (*a*) Section LXVIII. refers to the poet's grief as the trouble of his *youth* :

> It is the trouble of my youth
> That foolish sleep transfers to thee.

(*b*) The section which describes the visit to Cambridge (LXXXVII.), and contrasts the 'boys that crash'd the glass and beat the floor' with the

---

[1] He writes as though he had seen none of the poems before 1845. Can a word like 'just' have been omitted before 'finished'?

friends who once held debate in the same room, seems to imply a considerable lapse of time since the poet's Cambridge days. (*c*) The pathetic lines in XC.,

> Ah dear, but come thou back to me :
> Whatever change the years have wrought,
> I find not yet one lonely thought
> That cries against my wish for thee,

and (*d*) the phrase in CXIX., 'think of early days and thee,' appear to point in the same direction ; as does (*e*) the tone of a good many of the concluding sections of *In Memoriam.* In addition it may be observed (*f*) that, where a section shows a marked resemblance in idea or phrase to a passage in *The Princess* (1847), this may be significant as to date, and (*g*) that, if the resemblance in XLI. to a passage in *Zanoni* is not a coincidence, that section must be as late as 1842. On the other hand, in the Prologue we have the lines, which in strictness should refer to the whole poem,

> Forgive these wild and wandering cries,
> Confusions of a wasted youth ;

and the Epilogue (1842) speaks of that change

> Which makes appear the songs I made
> As echoes out of weaker times (21, 22).

Our results, it must be confessed, are meagre.

We know that certain sections were written soon after Arthur Hallam's death. We have good grounds for believing that certain others belong to the years 1836-37. One or two we can date about 1840, and we have reason to think that a good many fall between that year and the publication of the poem. But the natural inference from the words in the Prologue and the Epilogue is that the bulk of *In Memoriam* belongs to a time separated by some distance from 1849 and even from 1842. Beyond this we cannot go. We have no right to assume that a section which comes early in the poem was written early, or that a section which comes late was written late; though we can hardly help thinking it improbable that many of the last thirty or forty sections were composed within a few years of Hallam's death. Nor is our ignorance of the least consequence for the understanding of the poem. What is of consequence is the order in which the sections now stand. For although the poet 'did not write them with a view of weaving them into a whole,' he found that when they were written they were capable of being thus woven into a whole; and it seems quite clear that he endeavoured, by arrangement and probably by writing new pieces, to give the collection a certain amount of definite and significant structure. The result is that *In Memoriam*, though not one poem as *Lycidas* is one poem, is more than mere 'Fragments of an Elegy' (the title once thought of by the author, *Memoir*, I. 293), and justifies the name by which he sometimes referred to it, 'The Way of the Soul' (*ib.* 393). To fail to observe the changes in this 'Way' is to miss a great part of the meaning and beauty of *In Memoriam.*

III.

THE STRUCTURE OF *IN MEMORIAM*.

I. THE most obvious sign of definite structure in *In Memoriam* consists in the internal chronology, and it will be well to begin by making this clear.

Tennyson [1] himself tells us (*Memoir*, I. 305) that the divisions of the poem are made by the Christmas-tide sections (XXVIII., LXXVIII., CIV.). That the first of these refers to the first Christmas after the death of the friend in autumn is evident from XXX., 14-16 :

> We sung, tho' every eye was dim,
> A merry song we sang with him
> *Last year* : [2]

[1] It will be understood that generally, both in this Introduction and in the Notes, when I speak of 'the poet' I mean the poet who speaks *in* the poem. I refer to the author who composed the poem as 'Tennyson' or 'the author.'

[2] These lines are decisive, and their evidence is not weakened by the fact that some poems referring to the burial precede this

and we certainly receive the impression from the other Christmas poems that the second refers to the Christmas of the next year, and the third to that of the next again. Thus, when we have reached section CIV., we are distant from the death of the friend about two years and a quarter; and there is nothing in the sections after CIV. to make us think that they are supposed to cover any length of time. Accordingly, the time imagined to elapse in the poem may be set down as rather less than three years.

These results are confirmed by other facts. Between the Christmas poems there come occasional sections indicating the progress of time by reference to the seasons and to the anniversaries of the death of the friend; and between two Christmas poems we never find a hint that more than one spring or one summer has passed, or that more than one anniversary has come round. After the third Christmas we have a spring poem (CXV.), but after this no sign of summer or of the return of the anniversary of the friend's death.

first Christmas section, whereas the burial of Arthur Hallam did not really take place until after Christmas, 1833. The author did not choose to make the internal chronology coincide with the actual order of events.

The unmistakable indications of the internal chronology are shown in the following table:

Section	XI.	Early Autumn.
	XV.	Later.
	XXVIII.-XXX.	Christmastide.
	XXXVIII.-IX.	Spring.
	LXXII.	Anniversary.
	LXXVIII.	Christmastide.
	LXXXIII.	Delaying Spring.[1]
	LXXXVI., LXXXVIII.	Spring.
	LXXXIX., XCV., XCVIII.	Summer.
	XCIX.	Anniversary.
	CIV., CV.	Christmastide.
	CVI.	New Year's Day.
	CVII.	Winter.
	CXV., CXVI.	Spring.

Against all these indications there seems nothing to be set except the few passages already noted, where a phrase or the tone of a section appears to be not quite in harmony with this internal chronology. That these passages are so few is a proof of the care taken by the author to preserve the clearness and consistency of the scheme. And it is undoubtedly of use in giving the outlines of a structure to the poem, and of still greater use in providing beautiful contrasts between the sections which deal with the recurring seasons and anniversaries; though it is somewhat unfortunate that

[1] That this is not a New Year's Day poem is shown in the Notes.

the contents of some of the final sections imply a greater distance of time from the opening of the series than is suggested by the chronological scheme.

II. If we describe in the most general terms the movement of thought and feeling in *In Memoriam*, the description will be found to apply also to *Lycidas* or *Adonais*.   In each case the grief of the opening has passed at the close into triumph : at first the singer thinks only of loss and death, and at last his eyes are fixed upon the vision of a new and greater life.   But in *Lycidas* and *Adonais* this change is expressed in one continuous strain, and is therefore felt by the reader to occupy but a few hours of concentrated experience ; and in *Adonais* especially the impression of passionate rapidity in the transition from gloom to glory is essential to the effect.   In *In Memoriam* a similar change is supposed to fill a period of some years, and the impression of a very gradual and difficult advance is no less essential.   It is conveyed, of course, not only by the indications of time which have just been considered, but by the mere fact that each of the 131 sections is, in a sense, a poem complete in itself and accordingly felt to be the expression of the thought of one particular time.

In many cases, however, we soon observe that a single section is not really thus independent of its predecessor and successor. On the contrary, some are scarcely intelligible if taken in isolation ; and again and again we discover groups which have one subject, and in which the single sections are devoted to various aspects of this one subject. The poet in his progress has come upon a certain thought, which occupies him for a time and is developed through a series of stages or contrasted with a number of other thoughts. And even in cases where we cannot trace such a close connection in thought we often find that several consecutive sections are bound together, and separated from the poems that surround them, by a common tone of feeling. These groups or clusters correspond with single paragraphs of *Lycidas*, or with single stanzas or groups of stanzas in *Adonais* ; and their presence forms a second means by which a certain amount of structure is given to the poem.

There are many readers of *In Memoriam* who have never read the poem through, but probably everyone who has done so has recognised to some extent the existence of groups. Everyone remarks, for instance, that near the beginning there are a number of sections referring to the coming of the ship, and that there are other consecutive poems which deal with Christmastide. But perhaps few readers are aware of the large part played by these groups. The fact is that, taken together, they account for considerably more than one-half of the poem ; and in this estimate no notice has been taken of mere pairs of connected sections, such as XIX., XX. ; XLVIII., XLIX. ; LVII., LVIII. ; CXV., CXVI. ; or of parts of the poem where the sections, though not so closely connected as to form a distinct group, are yet manifestly united in a looser way. If these additions are made to our estimate, it will be found to include nearly 100 poems out of the total of 131.

Of the remaining sections (a) a small number may properly be called occasional poems, though the positions which they occupy in the whole are always more or less significant. Such are LXXXVII., which describes the visit to Cambridge ; XCVIII., on the brother's tour to Vienna ; the long retrospective poem, LXXXV. ; or the poem on Hallam's birthday, CVII. (b) Others at once remind us of preceding sections suggested by a like occasion, and in this way bring home to us the change which has taken place in the poet's mind during the interval. The Christmas poems are the most prominent instance; the later spring poems recall the earlier; the second 'Risest thou thus' brings back the first; the two sections beginning, 'Dark house,' and the two poems on the Yew-tree, form similar pairs. (*c*) Lastly, we find that the sections which immediately follow connected groups are often of one and the same kind. The subject which has occupied the poet's thoughts being dismissed, there follows a kind of reaction. He looks inward, and becomes more keenly conscious of the feeling from which his attention had been for the time diverted (*e.g.* XXXVIII.), or of the feeling in which his thoughts have culminated (*e.g.* LVII.). Not seldom this feeling suggests to him some reflection on his own songs: his singing comforts him on his dreary way, or he feels that it is of no avail, or that it expresses nothing of his deepest grief. And not only thus at the close of groups, but at various other points throughout *In Memoriam* there occur sections in which the poet's songs form the subject, pointing backwards and forwards to one another, and showing the change which passes over his mind as time goes on (*e.g.* V., XXI., LVIII., CXXV.). In these various ways, as well as by the presence of definite groups, some kind of connection is established between section and section almost throughout the whole of the poem.

III. We are now in a position to observe the structure of this whole, reserving for the Commentary the fuller characterisation of particular parts.

The 'Way of the Soul' we find to be a journey from the first stupor and confusion of grief, through a growing acquiescence often disturbed by the recurrence of pain, to an almost unclouded peace and joy. The anguish of wounded love passes into the triumph of love over sorrow, time and death. The soul, at first almost sunk in the feeling of loss, finds itself at last freed from regret and yet strengthened in affection. It pines no longer for the vanished hand and silent voice; it is filled with the con-sciousness of union with the spirit. The world, which once seemed to it a mere echo of its sorrow, has become the abode of that immortal Love, at once divine and human, which includes the living and the dead.

Is it possible to find in this 'Way' any turning-point where grief begins to yield to joy,—such a turning-point as occurs in *Adonais* when indignation rouses the poet from his sorrow, and the strain suddenly rises into the solemn affirmation,

'Peace, peace! he is not dead, he doth not sleep.'

If so, *In Memoriam* may be considered to fall into two fairly distinct parts, though the dividing-line would not necessarily come, any more than in *Adonais*, at the centre of the poem.

It might seem natural to take the long section LXXXV. as marking such a line of division, for here the poet himself looks back over the way he has traversed, and when he renews his journey the bitterness of grief seems to have left him.   But the passing away of this bitterness has been already clearly observable before section LXXXV. is reached, and the change of tone after that section does not seem sufficiently decided to justify us in regarding it as a central point in the whole.

More tempting would be a proposal to consider section LVII. as marking the centre of *In Memoriam*.   In these verses the most troubled and passionate part of the poem reaches the acme of a climax, while after them there is, on the whole, a steady advance towards acquiescence. But in reality the distress which culminates in section LVII. is characteristic only of the group which closes with that section ; it is not a distress which has deepened from the outset of the poem ; indeed, many tokens of advance have been visible before that group is reached, and the main direction of the movement towards it is definitely upward.[1]

If a turning-point in the general feeling of *In Memoriam* is to be sought at all, it must certainly be found not in section LVII., nor in section LXXXV., but in the second Christmas poem, LXXVIII. It seems true that, in spite of gradual change, the tone of the poem so far is, on the whole, melancholy, while after LXXVIII. the predominant tone can scarcely be called even sad; it is rather the feeling of spring emerging slowly and with difficulty from the gloom of winter. And it is probable that Tennyson himself intended this change to be associated with the second coming of Christmas, since the first and the third coming also announce a definite change,

[1] I am not converted, therefore, by Mr. Beeching's words, which have appeared since the above was written : ' Here the poem, as at first designed, seems to have ended. The 57th elegy [58th in the copyright text] represents the Muse as urging the poet to a new beginning ; and the 58th [59th] was added in the fourth edition, as though to account for the difference in tone between the earlier and later elegies' (Introduction, p. x). Apart from the objection urged above, the first sentence here seems to be scarcely consistent with Tennyson's own account of the composition of *In Memoriam*, nor can I believe that he ever thought of ending his poem in tones of despair. But it is certainly true that there is a more marked *break* at Section LVII. than at LXXVIII. or LXXXV. (The suggestion that the poem was originally intended to cease with LVII. was made in 1892 by Mr. Jacobs (p. 92), whose book was not known to Mr. Beeching.)

and since he says that the divisions of *In Memoriam* are made by the Christmas sections. At the same time it is questionable whether the transition at section LXXVIII. is so marked as to strike a reader who was not looking for signs of transition ; and, this being so, it would seem to be a mistake to regard *In Memoriam* as a poem which, like *Adonais*, shows a dividing line clearly separating one part of the whole from the other. Its main movement is really one of advance almost from the first, though the advance is for a long time very slow.

Falling back, then, on the divisions pointed out by the author, we may attempt to characterise the four parts into which the poem will fall, to show the groups contained in each, and to indicate the principal changes in the course of ideas through which the mind of the poet moves.

PART I. TO THE FIRST CHRISTMAS.
SECTIONS I.–XXVII.

The general tone of this part, which is supposed to cover a space of about three months, is that of absorption in grief ; but the poet gradually rises from mere suffering to a clearer conviction that

> 'Tis better to have loved and lost
> Than never to have loved at all,

and that love may, and ought to, survive the loss of the beloved. There is throughout scarcely any reference to the continued existence of the lost friend.

This part contains two distinct groups :

(1) Sections IX.-XVII. (or XX.),[1] referring to the coming of the ship (or to this and to the burial).

(2) Sections XXII.-XXV., a retrospect of the years of friendship.

Part II. To the Second Christmas.

Sections XXVIII.-LXXVII.

This part of the poem has some marked characteristics. (*a*) From beginning to end the idea of the continued life of the dead is prominent, far more prominent than in any of the other three parts. (*b*) It is through reflection on this idea and on the problems suggested by it that the poet wins his way forward ; so that this is the part of *In Memoriam* which contains most semi-philosophic speculation. (*c*) Hence this part consists almost wholly of distinct groups with intervening sections, and there are but few ' occasional ' poems.

---

[1] Here, as in a few other cases, it is a matter of doubt, and even of indifference, at which of two sections the group is best taken to close.

The following brief analysis of the groups will indicate the course of the poet's thoughts :

(1) Sections XXVIII.-XXX. Christmastide. The thought of the continued life of the dead emerges in an hour of exaltation.

(2) Sections XXXI.-XXXVI. This continued life is at once a 'truth revealed,' and a fact implied in the constitution of human nature. The group accordingly is concerned in part with the difference between two forms of faith in immortality.

(3) Sections XL.-XLVII. Immortality being assumed, the question of future reunion is raised. This involves the question (which is the main subject of the group) whether the earthly life is remembered beyond death. Only an affirmative answer would satisfy the demand of love.

(4) Sections L.-LVI. The poet's desire that the dead friend should remember him and be near him *now* (as well as in a future life) is followed by fears and doubts raised by the thought, first, of his own unworthiness, and then of all the pain, waste, and evil in the world. These doubts cannot be silenced by reason ; and the poet's hope that good is the end of evil, and love the

law of creation, is sustained only by blind trust.

(5) Sections LX.-LXV.   The poet returns to his desire that his friend should think of him *now*.   His hopes and fears on this subject are free from the distress of the preceding group, and issue in the acceptance of ignorance, and in faith that love cannot be lost.   Here, and in the remainder of Part II., there is a gradual advance towards quiet regret, sympathy with others, and a peaceful recognition of the beauty of the past and the influence of the lost friend.

(6) Sections LXVII.-LXXI.   On Night, Sleep, and Dreams.

(7) Sections LXXIII.-LXXVII.   On Fame.   The poet writes of his friend's loss of fame on earth and gain of fame in another world, and of the brevity of any fame which his own songs could win for his friend.

PART III.   TO THE THIRD CHRISTMAS.

SECTIONS LXXVIII.–CIII.

Of the four parts this contains the greatest number of sections which may be called 'occasional.' The idea of the future life retires again into the background.

(1) The prevailing tone of sections LXXIX.-LXXXIX. (not to be considered a group) is that of quiet and not unhappy retrospection, and a sense of new and joyful life begins to appear.

(2) Sections XC.-XCV. form a closely connected group on the possible contact of the living and the dead. The idea is considered from various sides, and appears to be realised in the trance recorded in XCV.

(3) Sections C.-CIII. form a group which has for its subject the poet's farewell to the home of childhood. He begins to turn his eyes from the past.

PART IV. FROM THE THIRD CHRISTMAS.

SECTIONS CIV.–CXXXI.

Throughout this part, even when the poet is thinking of the past, he is looking forward into the future. Regret is passing away, but love is growing and widening. The dead friend is regarded not only as a friend, but as a type of the nobler humanity to come, and as mingled with that Love which is the soul of the universe.

(1) Sections CIV.-CVI. form a group dealing with Christmas and New Year in the new home.

(2) Sections CVII., CVIII. express the poet's resolve to turn from the grief of the past.

(3) Sections CIX.-CXIV. describe the character of the dead friend, and incidentally the dangers of the progress of mankind.

(4) Sections CXVII.-CXXXI. are not so closely connected as to form a group, but they are united by their expression of faith in the future both of the individual and of humanity. In form many of them are retrospective, the poet looking back to the struggles through which he has won his way to entire faith in the omnipotence of love.[1]

[1] In conversation with Mr. James Knowles, Tennyson gave a division of *In Memoriam* into nine parts, as follows : (1) I.-VIII. ; (2) IX.-XX. ; (3) XXI.-XXVII. ; (4) XXVIII.-XLIX. ; (5) L.-LVIII. ; (6) LIX.-LXXI. ; (7) LXXII.-XCVIII. ; (8) XCIX.-CIII. ; (9) CIV.-CXXXI. As nothing is said of this arrangement in his notes on *In Memoriam* printed in the *Memoir*, it is to be supposed that he was not satisfied with it. It ignores the Second Christmas poem.

IV.

THE 'WAY OF THE SOUL.'

IT is a fashion at present to ascribe the great popularity of *In Memoriam* entirely to the 'teaching' contained in it, and to declare that its peculiar position among English elegies has nothing to do with its poetic qualities. This is equivalent to an assertion that, if the so-called substance of the poem had been presented in common prose,[1] the work would have gained the same hold upon the mass of educated readers that is now possessed by the poem itself. Such an assertion no one would make or consciously imply. The ordinary reader does not indeed attempt to separate the poetic qualities of a work from some other quality that appeals to him; much less does he read the work in terror of

[1] This, in strictness, is an impossible supposition. Anything that could be so presented would not be really the substance of the poem.

being affected by the latter; but imagination and diction and even versification can influence him much as they influence the people who talk about them, and he would never have taken *In Memoriam* to his heart if its consoling or uplifting thoughts had not also touched his fancy and sung in his ears. It is true, however, that he dwells upon these thoughts, and that the poem is often valued by him for its bearing upon his own life; and true again that this is one reason why he cares for it far more than for elegies certainly not inferior to it as poems. And perhaps here also many devotees of poetry may resemble him more than they suppose.

This peculiar position of *In Memoriam* seems to be connected with two facts. In the first place, it alone among the most famous English elegies is a poem inspired by deep personal feelings. Arthur Hallam was a youth of extraordinary promise, but he was also 'dear as the mother to the son.' The elegy on his death, therefore, unlike those on Edward King or Keats or Clough, bears the marks of a passionate grief and affection; and the poet's victory over sorrow, like his faith in immortality, is felt to be won in a struggle which has shaken the centre of his being. And then, as has been observed already,

the grief and the struggle are portrayed in all
their stages and phases throughout months and
years ; and each is depicted, not as it may have
appeared when the victory was won, but as it
was experienced then and there. In other elegies
for example, scarcely anything is to be found re-
sembling the earlier sections, which describe with
such vividness and truth the varied feelings of a
new grief; scarcely anything, again, like the night-
poems (LXVII. ff.), or the poem of the second
anniversary (XCIX.), or those of the third spring-
time (CXV., CXVI.). Stanzas like these come home
to readers who never cared for a poem before, and
were never conscious of feeling poetically till
sorrow opened their souls. Thus much of *In
Memoriam* is nearer to ordinary life than most
elegies can be, and many such readers have found
in it an expression of their own feelings, or have
looked to the experience which it embodies as a
guide to a possible conquest over their own loss.
' This,' they say to themselves as they read, ' is
what I dumbly feel. This man, so much greater
than I, has suffered like me and has told me how
he won his way to peace. Like me, he has been
forced by his own disaster to meditate on " the
riddle of the painful earth," and to ask whether the
world can really be governed by a law of love, and

is not rather the work of blind forces, indifferent to the value of all that they produce and destroy.'

A brief review, first of the experience recorded in *In Memoriam*, and then of the leading ideas employed in it, may be of interest to such readers, and even to others, as it may further the understanding of the poem from one point of view, although it has to break up for the time that unity of substance and form which is the essence of poetry.

The early sections portray a soul in the first anguish of loss. Its whole interest is fixed on one thing in the world ; and, as this thing is taken away, the whole world is darkened. In the main, the description is one of a common experience, and the poem shows the issue of this experience in a particular case.

Such sorrow is often healed by forgetfulness. The soul, flinching from the pain of loss, or apprehensive of its danger, turns away, at first with difficulty, and afterwards with increasing ease, from the thought of the beloved dead. 'Time,' or the incessant stream of new impressions, helps it to forget. Its sorrow gradually perishes, and with its sorrow its love ; and at last 'all it was is overworn,' and it stands whole and sound. It is not cynical to say that this is a

frequent history, and that the ideas repelled in
section XC. are not seldom true.

Sometimes, again, the wound remains unhealed,
although its pain is dulled.   Here love neither
dies nor changes its form; it remains a painful
longing for something gone, nor would anything
really satisfy it but the entire restoration of that
which is gone.   All the deeper life of the soul is
absorbed in this love, which from its exclusively
personal character is unable to coalesce with other
interests and prevents their growth.

In neither of these extreme cases is there that
victory of which the poet thinks, even in the first
shock of loss, when he remembers how it has been
said

> That men may rise on stepping-stones
> Of their dead selves to higher things.

In the first case there is victory of a kind, but it
is a victory which in the poet's eyes is defeat;
the soul may be said to conquer its sorrow, but it
does so by losing its love; it is a slave in the
triumph of Time.   In the second case, the 'self'
refuses to die and conquers time, but for that very
reason it is bound to the past and unable to rise
to higher things.   The experience portrayed in
In Memoriam corresponds with neither case, but
it resembles each in one particular.   Sorrow is

healed, but it is not healed by the loss of love : for the beloved dead is the object of continual thought, and when regret has passed away love is found to be not less but greater than before. On the other hand regret does pass away, and love does not merely look forward to reunion with its object but unites freely with other interests. It is evident that the possibility of this victory depends upon the fact that, while love does not die, there is something in the soul which does die. The self 'rises' only on the basis of a 'dead self.' In other words, love changes though it does not perish or fade ; and with the change in it there is a corresponding change in the idea of its object. The poem exhibits this process of two-fold change.

At the beginning love desires simply that which was, the presence and companionship of the lost friend ; and this it desires unchanged and in its entirety. It longs for the sight of the face, the sound of the voice, the pressure of the hand. These doubtless are desired as tokens of the soul ; but as yet they are tokens essential to love, and that for which it pines is the soul as known and loved through them. If the mourner attempts to think of the dead apart from them, his heart remains cold, or he recoils : he finds that he is thinking of a phantom ; 'an awful thought'

instead of 'the human-hearted man he loved';
'a spirit, not a breathing voice.' This he does
not and cannot love. It is an object of awe, not
of affection ; the mere dead body is a thousand-
fold dearer than this,—naturally, for this is not
really a spirit, a thinking and loving soul, but a
ghost. As then he is unable to think of the
object of his love except as 'the hand, the lips,
the eyes,' and 'the meeting of the morrow,' he
feels that what he loves is simply gone and lost,
and he finds his one relief in allowing fancy to
play about the thought of the tokens that remain
(see the poems to the ship).

The process of change consists largely in the
conquest of the soul over its bondage to sense.
So long as this bondage remains, its desire is fixed
on that which really is dead, and it cannot
advance. But gradually it resigns this longing,
and turns more and more to that which is not
dead. The first step in its advance is the
perception that love itself is of infinite value and
may survive the removal of the sensible presence
of its object. But no sooner has this conviction
been reached and embraced (XXVII.) than suddenly
the mourner is found to have transferred his
interest from the sensible presence to the soul
itself, while, on the other hand, the soul is no

longer thought of as a mere awful phantom, but
has become what the living friend had been,
something both beloved and loving (xxx.). This
conquest is, indeed, achieved first in a moment
of exaltation which cannot be maintained; but
its result is never lost, and gradually strengthens.
The feeling that the soul of the dead is something
shadowy and awful departs for ever, and step by
step the haunting desire for the bodily presence
retires. Thought is concentrated on that which
lives, the beauty of the beloved soul, seen in its
remembered life on earth, and doubtless shown
more fully elsewhere in a life that can be dimly
imagined. At last the pining for what is gone
dies completely away, but love is found to be but
stronger for its death, and to be no longer a source
of pain. It has grown to the dimensions of its
object, and this object is not only distant and
desired, but also present and possessed. And
more—the past (which is not wholly past, since it
lives and acts in the soul of the mourner) has lost
its pang and retained its loveliness and power:
'the days that are no more' become a life in death
instead of a 'death in life'; and even the light of
the face, the sound of the voice, and the pressure
of the hand, now that the absorbing desire for
them is still, return in the quiet inward world.

Another aspect of this change is to be noticed. So long as the mourner's sorrow and desire are fixed on that which dies they withdraw his interest from all other things. His world seems to depend for its light on that which has passed away, and he cries, ' All is dark where thou art not.' But as his love and its object change and grow, this exclusiveness lessens and its shadow shrinks. His heart opens itself to other friendships ; the sweet-ness of the spring returns ; and the 'mighty hopes' for man's future which the friend had shared, live again as the dead friend ceases to be a silent voice and becomes a living soul. Nor do the reviving activities simply flourish side by side with love for this soul, and still less do they compete with it. Rather they are one with it. The dead man lives in the living, and ' moves him on to nobler ends.' It is at the bidding of the dead that he seeks a friendship for the years to come. His vision of the ideal man that is to be is a memory of the man that trod this planet with him in his youth. He had cried, ' All is dark where thou art not,' and now he cries,

> Thy voice is on the rolling air ;
>   I hear thee where the waters run ;
>   Thou standest in the rising sun,
> And in the setting thou art fair.

For the sake of clearness little has been so far said of the thoughts of the mourner regarding the life beyond death. These thoughts touch two main subjects, the hope of reunion, and the desire that the dead friend should think of the living and should even communicate with him. The recurrent speculations on the state of the dead spring from this hope and this desire. They recur less frequently as the soul advances in its victory. This does not mean that the hope of reunion diminishes or ceases to be essential to the mourner's peace and faith ; but speculation on the nature both of this reunion and of the present life of the dead is renounced, and at last even abruptly dismissed (CVII., CVIII.). The singer is content to be ignorant and to wait in faith.

It is not quite so with the desire that the dead friend should now remember the living, and should even communicate with him. True, this desire is at one moment put aside without unhappiness (LXV.), and it ceases to be an urgent and disturbing force. But long after the pining for the bodily presence has been overcome, it remains and brings with it pain and even resentment. It seems to change from a hope of ‘ speech ’ or ‘ converse ’ to a wish that the dead should in some way be ‘ near ’ to or ‘ touch ’ the living ; and thus

it suggests the important group of sections
XC.-XCV. Here the poet even wishes at first for
a vision; and although he at once reflects that
neither this nor any other appeal to sense could
convince him that the dead was really with him,[1]
he does not surrender either here or later (CXXII.)
the idea of some more immediate contact of souls.[2]
On the other hand, he is not sure that the idea is
realised, nor does his uncertainty disturb his
peace. What he desires while he remains on
earth is contact with 'that which is,' the reality
which is half revealed and half concealed by
nature and man's earthly life, and which, by its
contact, convinces him of the reason and love that
rule the world; and, as now he thinks of his
friend as 'living in God,' he neither knows nor
seeks to know whether that which touches him is
to be called the soul of his friend or by some
higher name.

It appears then that the victory over sorrow
portrayed in the poem is dependent upon a

[1] His reflections on the difficulty or impossibility of any such
proof are expressed in XCII. with a conciseness which is characteristic of Tennyson and conceals from many readers the full force
and bearing of his thoughts.

[2] This idea is not confined to *In Memoriam*. Tennyson, we are
told, thought 'that there might be a more intimate communion than
we could dream of between the living and the dead, at all events for
a time' (*Memoir*, I. 320).

change in the love felt by the living for the dead, and upon a corresponding change in the idea of the dead. And some readers may even be inclined to think that the change is so great that at last the dead friend has really ceased to be to the living an individual person. He is, they will say, in some dim fashion 'mixed with God and Nature,' and as completely lost in 'the general soul' as is Adonais in Shelley's pantheistic poem : and so the poet's love for him has not merely changed, it has perished, and its place has been taken by a feeling as vaguely general and as little personal as the object to which it is directed. As my purpose is neither to criticise nor to defend the poet's ideas, but simply to represent them, I will confine myself to pointing out that the poem itself flatly denies the charge thus brought against it, and by implication denies the validity of the antitheses on which the charge rests. It is quite true that, as the poet advances, he abandons all attempts to define the life beyond death, and to form an image of his friend, 'whate'er he be.' It is quite true also that he is conscious that his friend, at once human and divine, known and unknown, far and near, has become something 'strange,' and is 'darklier understood' than in the old days of earthly life. But it is equally clear that to the poet his friend is not a whit less himself because he is 'mixed with God and Nature,' and that he is only 'deeplier loved' as he becomes 'darklier understood.'   And if the hope of reunion is less frequently expressed as the sense of present possession gains in strength, there is nothing in the poem to imply that it becomes less firm as the image of reunion becomes less definite.   The reader may declare that it ought to do so ; he may apply to the experience here portrayed his customary notions of human and divine, personal and impersonal, individual and general ; and he may argue that whatever falls under one of these heads cannot fall under the other.   But whether his ideas and his argument are true or false, the fact is certain that for the experience portrayed in *In Memoriam* (and, it may be added, in *Adonais* also) they do not hold. For the poets the soul of the dead, in being mingled with nature, does not lose its personality ; in living in God it remains human and itself ; it is still the object of a love as 'personal' as that which was given to

> the touch of a vanished hand,
> And the sound of a voice that is still.

V.

THE IDEAS USED IN *IN MEMORIAM.*[1]

AN understanding of the poem may be furthered, and the necessity for detailed explanations of particular passages may be avoided, if we now raise the questions: How does Tennyson habitually think of the soul and its future, and on what does his faith appear to be based?

Here certain cautions must be borne in mind. In the first place we must distinguish between that which is all-important and that which is of secondary interest. For example, it is evident that to Tennyson the fact of immortality was both certain and essential; but his ideas as to the precise nature of the future life or lives stand on

---

[1] In the following pages I have not attempted to maintain the distinction between 'Tennyson' and 'the poet' who speaks in his poetry; but it must be remembered that one has not in strictness a right to regard as an author's own opinion any statement he may make in a poem.

another level. It is useful to review these ideas, because they show us the world in which his imagination was accustomed to move; but they were not to him matters either of certainty or of great practical import. And, in the second place, we have to remember that Tennyson neither was nor professed to be a philosopher, and we must not expect from him either the exactness of language or the form of consecutive reasoning which are required in philosophy. In one section of *In Memoriam* (XLVIII.) he disclaims the intention of dealing fully or even seriously with the problems on which he has touched. Up to the time when he finished the poem he does not appear to have made any study of philosophers; and though a few of his later poems bear marks of some reading of this kind, and even employ terms too technical for poetry, in general the language remains that of imagination, and the form of argumentation or strict statement is never adopted. The reader, therefore, must not expect system or definition; he must not press hardly on single phrases or sentences, but must use them in order to feel his way into the poet's mind.

(1) If we try to picture the soul's history, as Tennyson habitually imagines it, our first question

must be: When did this history begin? Sometimes, we find, he imagines a previous existence,
or more than one, in which the soul was either
embodied or else 'floated free'; and certain
strange longings and dim visions which haunt its
earthly life are regarded as faint recollections of a
previous state (so, *e.g.*, in *The Two Voices, The
Ancient Sage, Far, far away*). But much more
often, and in *In Memoriam* probably always,[1] the
earthly life is thought of as the first life of the
soul, which is then figured as coming from the
'deep' of a larger spiritual being, or as detaching
itself, or being detached, from the 'general soul.'
This process is coincident with, or the spiritual
complement of, certain changes in matter which
issue in the body of the soul;[2] and later, through
experience gained by means of this body, the soul
developes into self-consciousness or personality
(XLV.). That which is deepest and most real in it
is sometimes spoken of as will or free-will, to
Tennyson the 'main-miracle, apparently an act of
self-limitation by the Infinite, and yet a revelation
by Himself of Himself.'[3]

The life on earth need not be considered here.
At death the union of soul and body is dissolved.

---

[1] See on XLIV.   [2] See on CXX.
[3] *Memoir*, I. 316. Cf. *De Profundis*, and CXXXI.

The idea that thereupon the soul passes at once to a final state of bliss or woe, is on the whole foreign to the poet's mind, and is repudiated (in *The Ring*). So is the idea that at the end of the earthly life the soul at once remerges into the general soul so as to lose its individuality (XLVII.). And again the idea that at death the soul falls into a long sleep from which it will awake unchanged, though entertained as a possibility in XLIII., is evidently not habitual with the poet. He habitually imagines the soul as entering on a second individual life immediately after death. The new life is almost always, if not always, thought of as implying a new embodiment ; and sometimes, perhaps generally, this embodiment is supposed to take place on some other world or ' star.' The soul's second life, if it lived well on earth, is regarded as free from many of the limitations and defects of the first. Though occasionally described as though it were an existence of merely contemplative happiness, it is generally imagined as a life of activity in which the soul takes part in some common work and so advances on the path of progress. Usually, though not always, the poet thinks of the soul as remembering its past and its earthly companions ; occasionally he imagines it as being, at least for a time, peculiarly ' near ' to

the beloved on earth and perhaps even able to
'touch' them without the intervention of sense;
as a rule, and in *In Memoriam* habitually, he
thinks of a reunion and recognition, in the next
life, of souls dear to one another in this.

The second life is supposed to be succeeded by
death, on which follows a third embodied life; and
this process is repeated again and again for ages,
the soul in each embodiment reaching a higher
stage of being, and approaching more and more
nearly to God.[1]   The union with God in which
this progress would presumably terminate, the
poet naturally does not attempt to imagine; but
it is noticeable that, if we may judge from XLVII.
and the phrases quoted in *Memoir*, I. 319, the
idea of an *ultimate* 'absorption into the divine'
was not, like the idea of an immediate absorption,
repugnant to him; and perhaps with this we may
connect the fact that in the trance-experience
which he several times described, 'the loss of
personality (if so it were)' seemed to him 'no
extinction but the only true life' (*Memoir*, I. 320).
Of the future of souls which grew worse with time
in their earthly state he does not write, but, as his
later poems show, he could not entertain the belief
that any soul would in the end be excluded from

[1] See, *e.g.*, *De Profundis.*

a God of love.   The 'larger hope' of LV., and
perhaps the

> one far-off divine event
> To which the whole creation moves (Epilogue),

are phrases which refer to the final reconciliation
or union of all souls with their divine source.

(2) How many of the ideas just summarised
were to the poet matters of belief and of essential
importance we do not know; and therefore, in
turning to the question of the basis of his belief in
immortality, we must dismiss the greater part of
them, and must understand by 'immortality'
simply the conscious and indefinitely prolonged
life of the soul beyond death.   For this was to
him undoubtedly a matter of fixed belief, and of
an importance so great that life without the belief
in it seemed to him to have neither sense nor
value.   We must remember also that immortality
was to his mind a fact of the same order as the
existence of a God of love, so that what is said of
the grounds of his faith in the one may often be
taken to apply also to the grounds of his faith in
the other; and where the two ideas are not
regarded as thus coordinate, the belief in immortality is considered as a consequence of belief
in God, so that the basis of the latter is indirectly
also the foundation of the former.

In the first place, then, it is clear that God and immortality are to the poet matters not of knowledge or proof, but of faith.   Concerning them

> We have but faith : we cannot know ;
>   For knowledge is of things we see.

We embrace them ' by faith, and faith alone,'

> Believing where we cannot prove. (Cf. CXXXI.)

This position is maintained throughout Tennyson's poetry, and is set forth most fully and maturely in the following lines from *The Ancient Sage* :

> Thou canst not prove the Nameless, O my son,
> Nor canst thou prove the world thou movest in,
> Thou canst not prove that thou art body alone,
> Nor canst thou prove that thou art spirit alone,
> Nor canst thou prove that thou art both in one :
> Thou canst not prove thou art immortal, no
> Nor yet that thou art mortal—nay my son,
> Thou canst not prove that I, who speak with thee,
> Am not thyself in converse with thyself,
> For nothing worthy proving can be proven,
> Nor yet disproven : wherefore thou be wise,
> Cleave ever to the sunnier side of doubt,
> And cling to Faith beyond the forms of Faith !

The ideas of God and immortality, in the next place, are not for the poet the result of reasoning upon the phenomena of external Nature.   He appears to have held consistently throughout his life, that if we did not bring them with us to the examination of Nature, but simply used our reason upon it without taking into account the evidence derived from our own nature, we should not believe either in God or in immortality. As an undergraduate he voted No on the question raised in the Apostles' Society, Is an intelligible First Cause deducible from the phenomena of the universe ? [1] (*Memoir*, I. 44.) He would say, on looking through the microscope, 'Strange that these wonders should draw some men to God and repel others. No more reason in one than in the other' (*Ib.* 102). And so the poet in *In Memoriam* declares :

> I found Him not in world or sun,
>> Or eagle's wing, or insect's eye. (CXXIV.)

Nay, in his dark hour, it even seems to him that the message of Nature is a terrible one; that, 'red in tooth and claw with ravine,' she 'shrieks against his creed'; that the world is a process of ceaseless change, in which individual existences arise to pass without return ; that its forces show no token that they value life more than death, good more than evil, or the soul more than a grain of sand. And though these are but 'evil dreams' born of

[1] And 'an intelligible First Cause' is less than a 'God of love, or 'something that watches over us' (Tennyson's words to Mr. Knowles).

his distress,[1] and Nature appears to him far otherwise when he views it, as he habitually does, in the light of ideas derived from another source, he is still constant to the position that Nature, regarded by itself, would not convince him of immortality or God.

So far all is clear. And the positive question, Whence then, according to the poet, is the faith in these ideas derived? admits of an easy answer in general terms. ‘ Such ideas,’ he says, ‘ we get from ourselves, from what is highest within us ’ (*Memoir*, I. 314). But when we proceed to ask, What is this ‘ highest within us ’? we find difficulties, and it is certainly not safe to found an answer, as is often done, upon three or four lines in a single section of *In Memoriam*. Our best plan will rather be to collect and place in order some crucial passages from various poems, and then to elicit a result from them.

[1] The lines referred to, and similar lines, are often completely misunderstood. It is absurd to quote them as expressing Tennyson's habitual view of Nature, or as his description of the universe regarded by ‘ cold reason.’ They describe the world as regarded by a reason which is turning away from all the evidence afforded by human nature, and which is, moreover, being used hurriedly and in alarm. It is no less a misunderstanding to suppose Tennyson to say or hint that, even with *all* the evidence before it, reason draws conclusions hostile to the ideas of God and immortality : what he says is that reason cannot *prove* the truth of these ideas.

(*a*) In *The Two Voices* one voice pleads that the senses tell us ' the dead are dead.'   The poet answers :

> Who forged that other influence,
> That heat of inward evidence,
> By which [man] doubts against the sense?
>
> He owns the fatal gift of eyes,
> That read his spirit blindly wise,
> Not simple as a thing that dies.
>
> Here sits he shaping wings to fly :
> His heart forebodes a mystery :
> He names the name Eternity.
>
> That type of Perfect in his mind
> In Nature can he nowhere find.
> He sows himself on every wind.

This does not mean that he imposes his own fancies on the universe ; rather, these inward evidences are regarded as the witness of the power which reaches ' through Nature moulding men,' and ' revealing ' itself ' in every human soul ' (*Memoir*, II. 420).

(*b*) They are often said to come through feeling, or are called feeling. God, to the Ancient Sage, is

> That which knows
> And is not known, but felt thro' what we feel
> Within ourselves is highest.

And, in particular, as love is the highest we feel, we must believe that God is Love (*Memoir*, II.

377). So in *In Memoriam* (CXXIV.) the 'evil dreams' which Nature lends are opposed by feeling or the heart:

> A warmth within the breast would melt
>> The freezing reason's colder part,
>> And like a man in wrath the heart
> Stood up and answered 'I have felt';

and, in his distress, the poet cries to what he 'feels is Lord of all.' In *In Memoriam*, again, it is chiefly (though not solely) the presence of love within himself that makes the poet declare that, without immortality, life would be valueless, and man a monster, because combining the contradictory attributes of love and mortality: and in *Vastness* the similar passionate assertions that nothing in the world could matter if man were doomed to perish, are suddenly broken off with the words:

> Peace, let it be! for I loved him, and love him for ever: the dead are not dead but alive.

(*c*) Finally, in *The Two Voices* the poet appeals to mysterious intimations:

> Heaven opens inward, chasms yawn,
> Vast images in glimmering dawn,
> Half shown, are broken and withdrawn.
> .   .   .   .   .   .
> Moreover, something is or seems,
> That touches me with mystic gleams,
> Like glimpses of forgotten dreams.

So in the *Holy Grail* and the *Ancient Sage* reference is made to the inward evidence of exceptional
moments when everything material becomes un-
real or visionary, yet there is in the soul 'no
shade of doubt, But utter clearness,' and man

> feels he cannot die,
> And knows himself no vision to himself,
> Nor the high God a vision.[1]

And so, in *In Memoriam*, not only is this trancelike
experience one in which the soul comes 'on that
which is,' and for a moment seems to understand
the riddle of the world (XCV.), but the cry of distress
to what is felt as Lord of all is immediately followed
by the vision of the reality behind appearances :

> And what I am beheld again
> > What is, and no man understands. (CXXIV.)

If now we consider these various passages, what
answer do they give to our question concerning
the basis of the poet's faith ? They show at once
that it does not suffice to take the stanza ending
'I have felt,' and to reply : Tennyson thinks that
the emotions or 'heart' cannot be satisfied without
a belief in God and immortality, and that is the
sole ground of his belief. For this account of the

---

[1] *Holy Grail, sub fin.* I omit the following words, 'nor that One
Who rose again,' because the speaker is King Arthur, and because
this idea does not appear to be used as a source of evidence
elsewhere.

matter, even if it were satisfactory for one passage, evidently does not apply to others.   The 'highest within us' seems to be generally accompanied by emotion, but not always, or even generally, to be an emotion.   Often it is love, but it is obviously not so in the lines quoted from *The Two Voices*, nor apparently in those from the *Holy Grail* and the *Ancient Sage*; and love, to which the appeal is made in *In Memoriam*, XXXIV., XXXV., is coupled with other high activities and achievements in LVI., and is not referred to at all in the lines from XCV. or the last lines of CXXIV.   The 'highest within us' means many things, and its meaning could be further extended if we went beyond our list of passages.

Nor is the use made of this consciousness of a higher always the same.   It seems to be of two distinct kinds.   Sometimes the poet, looking at that which he feels to be highest in himself, finds it to point beyond earthly experience ; and on this characteristic of it he founds what is, in effect, an *argument* in favour of immortality or the divine origin of the soul.   So it is with the shaping of wings that yet can never fly on earth ; or the presence of the ideas of eternity and perfection which cannot be derived from mere nature nor realised here ; or the mysterious intimations of

The Two Voices.   So it is also with love, which
appears to the poet to imply in its very nature
the immortality both of itself and of its object.
To him the existence of these tokens of immortality in man, if it were coupled with the fact
of mortality, would make man an inexplicable
' monster,' and deprive both his life and the history
of the earth of all their meaning.   This then is
one way in which his consciousness of the best
within him yields a basis for the poet's faith ; and
when he replies to the freezing reason ' I have
felt,' the feeling he appeals to is not the desire to
be immortal, nor yet a feeling that he is immortal,
but the feeling of love, which he points to as a
fact inconsistent with the theory of the world put
forward in his dark mood by his reason.

But there is another way.   When King Arthur
says that there are moments when he *feels* he
cannot die ; when God is said to be *felt* through
what we feel within ourselves is highest ; when
the poet speaks of that which he *feels* is Lord of
all, there is a more direct appeal to something
called feeling.[1]   Here the poet does not point to

[1] With these passages, cf. the famous speech beginning ' Misshör '
mich nicht' in the scene *Marthens Garten* in *Faust*, Part I., and
also the contrast of feeling and ' the reasoning power ' in *The
Excursion*, Book IV., towards the end ('I have seen A curious
child,' etc.).

something within him which seems to imply immortality or God, and from which therefore these may be inferred ; the feelings of which he speaks are, or give, an immediate assurance of God or of immortality. It would probably be vain to attempt to define these ' feelings ' more exactly, or to ask whether the poet's meaning was simply that at certain moments, recognised by him as his highest, he was unable to doubt the exist- ence of God and immortality, or whether he meant that at these moments he appeared to himself to have a direct and positive apprehension of the soul as immortal, and of God as Love.[1] What is clear is that, on the one hand, these feelings are not merely what we generally call emotions, since a certainty of God and immortality is conveyed in them ; and that, on the other hand, the assurance they convey is direct or immediate, not dependent on reasoning or ' proof.' Such phrases, in the descriptions of the trance-like state, as ' *came on* that which is,' ' *beheld* what is,' ' *knows* himself no vision,' are evidently meant to indicate this same immediate certainty.

It is on the second of these two kinds of

---

[1] This certainly does seem to be implied or asserted in some of the phrases quoted, and especially in some which describe the trance- like experience.   But these phrases do not refer, at any rate explicitly, to immortality; nor is it safe to lay weight on them.

'inward evidence' that the poet seems to lay most stress. And the reason of this doubtless is that the first kind obviously involves a process of reasoning, and that to him this process is not accompanied by the conviction of certainty. It falls short of 'proof.' Thus in *The Two Voices* the presence in the soul of certain ideas, activities, and feelings, was taken to point to the divine origin and the immortality of that soul, but it did not give the 'assurance' for which the poet longed, and which came later when, at the sound of a mysterious inner voice which whispered hope,

> From out [his] sullen heart a power
> Broke, like the rainbow from the shower,
>
> To feel, altho' no tongue can prove,
> That every cloud, that spreads above
> And veileth love, itself is love.

In the same way it seems clear to him that a being who can love as he loves, and who yet is doomed to perish, is a 'monster,' a 'dream,' a 'discord'; but this does not give him *assurance* that the soul is not such a monstrosity. On the other hand the 'feelings' of which he speaks in the passages quoted, like the experience of the trance-like state, involve for him no process of inference, do not pretend to 'prove,' and do carry with them the 'assurance' he requires.

Indeed, the language used of these feelings and experiences is of such a kind that one is tempted to ask why, after all, the poet should declare that

> We have but faith : we cannot know ;
> For knowledge is of things we see:

since the immediate certainty claimed for these feelings would appear to be, or to justify, something more than faith or a believing of what we cannot prove.   Perhaps he distrusted what he could not suppose to be the common possession of mankind.   Or perhaps his answer would be found in Wordsworth's lines which tell us that it is

> the most difficult of tasks to *keep*
> Heights which the soul is competent to gain.

She gains them, he might say, in exceptional moments ; and the experience of these moments, when she is conscious of being at her best, becomes the light of her life.   But they come rarely, and they pass quickly away, or, it may be, are 'stricken thro' with doubt' (XCV.).   The soul sinks back and loses its contact with reality, and in the long intervals between these visits must rely on memory and hope, living in the assurance, not of vision or feeling, but of faith in what it once saw and felt.   This faith is not an adherence to something which reason declares false, but it is

E

an adherence to something which reason cannot prove to be true ; for that which can be 'known' or proved is always a limited and subordinate truth, while the 'systems and creeds' which strive to render intelligible to the soul the experience of her highest moments, lack on the one hand the 'assurance' of those moments themselves, and on the other hand the certainty of the lower truths which can be proven and are not 'worthy proving.'

VI.

A FEW words may be added on two purely literary matters.

One of these is the metre of *In Memoriam.* It is uncommon, and, so far as I am aware, no example of it has been found in English poetry prior to the Elizabethan Age. From that time down to Tennyson's it was occasionally used, how rarely may be judged from the brevity of the following list of instances, either of the metre itself or of a four-line four-accent stanza with the same disposition of rhymes : Sidney, *Astrophel and Stella,* Second Song (trochaic, with double rhymes in lines 1 and 4), and *Psalm* xxxvii. (double rhymes in lines 2 and 3) ; Shakespeare, *The Phœnix and Turtle* (trochaic) ; Jonson, *Underwoods,* xxxix. (*An Elegy*), and *Catiline,* Chorus in Act II.; Carew, *Separation of Lovers* (trochaic); Sandys, *Paraphrase of the Psalms,* Psalms 14, 30, 44, 74, 140 ; Lord Herbert of Cherbury, *An Ode upon a Question moved whether Love should con-*

tinue for ever; George Herbert, *The Temper* (lines
1 and 4 have five accents); Harvey's *Synagogue*,
1640 (I have not seen this); Marvell, *Daphnis
and Chloe* (trochaic); Prior, *To the Hon. Charles
Montague, Esquire* (version quoted in Thackeray's
Humourists)[1]; Somervile, *Fable* viii.; Langhorne,
An Ode to the Genius of Westmoreland; Robert
Anderson, *The Poor Prude* (Poems, Carlisle,
1820; I have not seen this); Landor, *Imaginary Conversations*, vol. 3, 1828, two stanzas in
'Landor, English Visiter, and Florentine Visiter.'[2]
Stanzas in two or three of these poems faintly
recall Tennyson's cadences to the ear, and there
have been theories as to the source whence he
derived the metre. He himself stated that he
believed himself the originator of it, until
after *In Memoriam* came out, when some one
told him that Ben Jonson and Sir Philip Sidney
had used it (*Memoir*, I. 305). This is decisive
as to Tennyson's belief, though not as to the
possibility of his having reproduced the metre of
some poem which he had forgotten.

[1] I have failed to find this version in editions of Prior. The two
usually printed have alternate rhymes. If Thackeray made the
version himself, it is doubtless later than *In Memoriam*.

[2] For the greater part of this list I am indebted to various sources,
notably Schipper's *Englische Metrik*. D. G. Rossetti's *My Sister's
Sleep* was published before *In Memoriam*, but after *You ask me why*
and *Love thou thy land*.

More interesting than the question where the
metre came from is the fact that in the early
poems we can see Tennyson feeling his way
towards it. It appears, though not in an independent form, in the volumes of 1830 and 1833.
Thus we find it in the second half of each stanza
of *Mariana* and *Mariana in the South*: *e.g.*,

> The broken sheds looked sad and strange:
> Unlifted was the clinking latch;
> Weeded and worn the ancient thatch
> Upon the lonely moated grange.

And the peculiar effect of the *In Memoriam* stanza
is quite perceptible in the following lines from the
poem beginning, *Clear-headed friend*:

> Low-cowering shall the Sophist sit;
> Falsehood shall bare her plaited brow;
> Fair-fronted Truth shall droop not now
> With shrilling shafts of subtle wit.
> Nor martyr-flames, nor trenchant swords
> Can do away that ancient lie;
> A gentler death shall Falsehood die,
> Shot thro' and thro' with cunning words.

Even earlier, in Alfred Tennyson's contributions
to the *Poems by Two Brothers* (1827), passages in
this metre occur; for example:

> The vices of my life arise,
> Pourtray'd in shapes, alas! too true;
> And not one beam of hope breaks through,
> To cheer my old and aching eyes (p. 20: cf. p. 23).

Again :

> Or had he seen that fatal night
>> When the young King of Macedon
>> In madness led his veterans on,
> And Thais held the funeral light,
> Around that noble pile which rose
>> Irradiant with the pomp of gold,
>> In high Persepolis of old,
> Encompass'd with its frenzied foes (p. 64: cf. p. 66).

Once more :

> The great, the lowly, and the brave
>> Bow down before the rushing force
>> Of thine unconquerable course ;
> Thy wheels are noiseless as the grave (p. 114).

The other subject on which a few words seem
to be required is Tennyson's indebtedness to other
poets.   I do not refer to such general influences
as that of Dante and, still more, Petrarch on the
ideas and sentiment of parts of *In Memoriam*, an
influence which Mr. Collins has pointed out and
which seems to be indisputable.   No one would
criticise the poet on this score.   But there are a
large number of phrases in *In Memoriam* which
recall the phrases of other poets, a larger number
than we should probably be able to find in the
same amount of verse by any other famous
English author except Milton and Gray.   It is
on the ground of these apparent borrowings that

Tennyson has been criticised ; and he seems to
have been sensitive to such criticism.

It is essential to distinguish the possible causes
of the similarities of phrase here in question.
Sometimes a poet adopts the phrase of an earlier
writer knowingly, and with the intention that
the reader should recognise it ; and if the reader
fails to recognise it he does not fully appreciate
the passage.   Milton and Gray often did this, and
Tennyson does it to beautiful effect when he reproduces phrases of Virgil or Theocritus ; and so
in *In Memoriam*, when he writes 'change their
sky' or 'brute earth' he means the Horatian
phrases to be recognised.   Sometimes, again, the
similarity of phrase is due to mere coincidence :
the second poet never read the words of the first,
but he invents for himself what the first had invented for himself.   A third cause is unconscious
reproduction : a phrase is retained in memory
perhaps for years, and is reproduced without any
consciousness that it is not perfectly original.
Lastly, a poet may use the words of a predecessor, knowing what he is doing but not intend-
ing the origin of the phrase to be observed.   This
is plagiarism, and it is the only one of the four
cases in which any discredit attaches to the poet.

We may dismiss the first and the last of these

cases. The interesting question is whether most of the 'borrowings' in Tennyson's poetry are to be regarded as coincidences or as reminiscences. The poet himself seems to have considered them to be the former, and scarcely to have realised that such a thing as unconscious reproduction exists. Probably in some minds its limits are well defined; but with other writers this is not so, and many a man of letters has often to endure the vexation of finding that a phrase which seemed particularly appropriate and came particularly easily was not his own property at all. Such writers are equally apt to reproduce phrases of their own without any suspicion that they are repeating themselves; and in general it is certain that unusual retentiveness of verbal memory may be combined with unusual unconsciousness that memory is being employed.

Now some of Tennyson's 'borrowings' are doubtless cases of mere coincidence, but it seems to me beyond doubt that a greater number are reminiscences, and that he was more than commonly subject to this trick of memory.[1]   The

[1] Sometimes he may have been aware of the reminiscence at the time of writing and have forgotten it afterwards. It is observable that in the *Poems by Two Brothers* he is scrupulous in acknowledging obligations (or boyishly anxious to show knowledge): *e.g.* he notes his debt to 'that famous chorus in Caractacus' (p. 116), or to

extent of his 'borrowings' is in favour of this view : why otherwise should his language happen to coincide with that of other poets so much more often than does the language, say, of Shelley or Keats ? Again, when there can be little doubt that he had read the passage of an earlier poet in which the phrase occurs, it is more probable that he reproduced this phrase than that he invented it. For example, if the words

> To seek the empty, vast, and wandering air

occurred in Middleton or Tourneur, we might naturally take Tennyson's

> Drops in his vast and wandering grave

for a mere coincidence ; but when we consider that the first of these lines comes from one of the most famous speeches in Shakespeare, we can have little doubt that the writer of the second had read this speech and was unknowingly borrowing from it. If a reader of the Prologue to *In*

'the songs of Jayadeva, the Horace of India' (p. 165). When (*ib.*) he adds to the line,

> And in th' ambrosia of thy smiles the god of rapture lay,

the note, 'Vide Horace's ODE—"Pulchris EXCUBAT in genis,"' he is not acknowledging an obligation but asking the reader to enjoy his line the more because it recalls Horace's word (our first case above). The reader of these poems of boyhood will soon convince himself that, from the first, Tennyson had a poet's feeling for phrases, and a very retentive memory of them.

Memoriam were reminded of only one passage in Herbert's *Temple*, he might be content with the hypothesis of coincidence; but when he is reminded of five distinct passages, and when in other parts of *In Memoriam* he is again reminded of Herbert, he can hardly doubt that he is dealing with reminiscences. Or, to take an example from *Crossing the Bar*, it is surely far more likely that the word 'moaning' in the line,

> And may there be no moaning of the bar,

is unconsciously due to Kingsley's

> And the harbour bar be moaning,

than that Tennyson had never read a song so famous as *The Three Fishers* and independently hit on the same word. This view, lastly, is greatly strengthened by the fact that Tennyson reproduces his own expressions. The following commentary may convince the reader of this fact, and I have no doubt that a Tennyson lexicon would make it still more patent. It is scarcely credible that most of these reproductions were conscious.[1] It is even probable that a poet so careful and so sensitive to criticism would have

---

[1] Those from poems unpublished or withdrawn may of course be so. For example, Tennyson seems to have used phrases from his early poem, *The Lover's Tale*, somewhat freely.

altered any passage in which he discovered that
he had repeated himself.

To take the view taken here is not to bring
a charge against Tennyson or to cast doubts on
his originality.   Indeed, to doubt his originality
in the creation of poetic phrases would be to
show the extreme of critical incapacity.   It is
quite possible to hold that in respect of thought
and inventive imagination he was not among the
most original of our poets ; but if ever poet were
a master of phrasing he was so, and the fact that
he was so is quite unaffected by the further fact
that he was sometimes unconsciously indebted to
his predecessors.

COMMENTARY.

PROLOGUE.

FOR purposes of study, this famous poem is best read after the sections of *In Memoriam* have been traversed; and the later sections, in particular, will be found the best commentary on it. Its connection with the whole work, however, may be indicated here.

In the first shock of grief the poet felt that the love within him was his truest self, and that it must not die. He clung to it through all his sorrow, and its demands formed a test by which he tried the doubts and fears that beset him. At the end he found that it had conquered time, outlived regret, and grown with his spiritual growth.

A like undying love he 'embraced,' even in his darkest hours, as 'God indeed' and 'Creation's final law.' He embraced it, however, through 'feeling' and by 'faith': he did not reach it by studying Nature, nor could he prove its existence. But at the end, when the love within him had reached its full stature, his faith in Love as the King and Lord of the universe had only become more fixed. And his friend, while 'deeplier loved,' had become mingled with this immortal Love, 'known and unknown, human, divine.'

In the Prologue this result of the poet's experience is summed up, and the connection of thought in the first eight stanzas may be shown, with the explicitness of prose, as follows. In stanza 1, immortal Love is addressed as the Son, or revelation, of God; invisible, unproveable, embraced by faith alone. The next stanzas tell us what, to this faith, immortal Love is. It is more than human, being the origin and the lord of all: of the world, of life, of death,—death, which it made and will annul (st. 2, 3). It is not merely divine, but human, and the perfection of humanity; not only, therefore, the origin and master of man's life, but the supreme end of his desire and will (st. 4). We cannot 'know' it—for its white light is refracted in our minds—but it is, we trust, the source of the knowledge that we have (st. 5, 6). And, therefore, our knowledge (which is not ours) should be mingled with reverence and humility (st. 7, 8).

It seems probable that Tennyson had been reading George Herbert shortly before writing these stanzas, for some of the coincidences of thought and phrase, pointed out by Collins, can hardly be accidental. Herbert's *Love*, for example, opens thus:

> Immortal Love, Author of this great frame,
>   Sprung from that beauty which can never fade,
> How hath Man parcell'd out Thy glorious name,
>   And thrown it on the dust which Thou hast made.

Cf. again with stanzas 2 and 3 the lines:

> Whether I fly with angels, fall with dust,
> Thy hands made both (*The Temper*),

and

> My God hath promised; He is just (*The Discharge*).

1. 'To enquiries as to the meaning of the words "Immortal Love" in the Introduction to *In Memoriam*, he explained that he had used "Love" in the same sense as St. John (1 John, chap. iv.)': *Memoir*, I. 312. Cf. Epilogue, 141.

4. Cf. LIV. 13, 14, LV. 17-20, CXXXI. 9, 10, and many passages in other poems; *e.g.* the lines quoted above, p. 55.

5. 'orbs of light and shade': orbs, such as earth, half light, half shade. Cf. 'This whole wide earth of light and shade,' *Will Waterproof*, and Gabriel's song in the Prologue to *Faust*. The 'light' and 'shade' are, however, not *merely* physical: Life is light, Death (as often in Tennyson) shadow. Both are 'thine.'

7 f. 'and lo,' etc.: and art lord of Death (cf. Macbeth's 'way to dusty death'). Line 9 continues the thought. There is probably a reminiscence of Rev. x. 2, a chapter which Tennyson 'would quote with boundless admiration' (*Memoir*, I. 279.)

11. Cf. LVI. 8-20, and see *Locksley Hall Sixty Years After* for the idea that the hope of immortality is well-nigh universal.

12. 'thou art just.' And would it have been just to make him merely that he might die? Is 'dust' to be his wages (see *Wages*)? Or perhaps, as has been suggested to me, the idea is rather: To make him such that he thinks himself immortal when he is really not so, would be unjust. The idea of a duty of submission to *mere* omnipotence is quite foreign to Tennyson, in whom Jowett remarked 'a strong desire to vindicate the ways of God to man, and, perhaps, to

F

demonstrate a pertinacity on the part of man in demanding
of God his rights' (*Memoir*, II. 464). Cf. 'redress' in LVI.
27, CVI. 12, 'sense of wrong' in LXXI. 7, 'wrath' in LXXXII.
14, 'bitterness' in LXXXIV. 47 ; also *By an Evolutionist*.

13-16. The thought seems to be : As 'immortal Love' is
not only divine (lines 5 ff.), but the perfection of that humanity
which is imperfect in us, it is to us the ideal or supreme will
with which we have to identify our wills. 'We know not
how' : for Tennyson's feeling about the 'main miracle' of
free will see on CXXXI. Cf. Browne, *Rel. Med.* I. 36, 'Thus
we are men, and we know not how,' and the context.

19. The metaphor is that of refraction, as in the famous
simile in *Adonais* :

> Life, like a dome of many-coloured glass,
> Stains the white radiance of eternity,
> Until Death tramples it to fragments.

Tennyson often employs it : *e.g.* in *Will Waterproof*, 'Ten
thousand broken lights and shapes, Yet glimpses of the
true'; cf. *The Higher Pantheism*, where he has also the
image of the 'straight staff bent in a pool.' When he calls
Christ 'that purest light of God' (*Memoir*, I. 169), the metaphor in 'purest' is the same.

25-28. Cf. CXIV. and notes. 'As before': 'before the
growth of knowledge disturbed their union,' rather than
simply 'as hitherto.'

31. 'to bear': to bear 'thy light,' *i.e.* the light of knowledge (23, 24), instead of supposing it to be their own and so
feeling a foolish pride. The notion of pride has suggested
the epithet in line 32 (cf. CXIV. 9).

32. 'worlds': Tennyson generally speaks as though he
believed in a number of inhabited worlds,

33-36. 'sin' surely does not refer specially to his grief (37),
nor 'worth' to his love (40). The meaning is more general,
as 'since I began' proves. 'What seemed' is an expression
of ignorance : 'what rightly or wrongly I distinguished as
my defects and my merits.' The latter equally need forgive-

ness ; for though there is 'merit' as between man and man, there is none as toward God.

37. Cf. LXXXV. 61, 62.

39. Cf. Epilogue, 140, and CXXIX., CXXX. ; also XXXII. 5-8, 14.

41. Cf. 'Wild words wander here and there,' *A Dirge.* 'Wild and wandering' occurs in *Troilus and Cressida*, I. i. 105 (Beeching). Cf. LVII. 4 (Robinson).

42. Cf. 'These dark confusions that within me rest,' Vaughan's *Dressing* (Collins). There is a curious coincidence with 'meos libros, seu verius confusiones,' Luther, Preface to vol. I. of his *Works*, 1545 (G. A. C.). 'Wasted': 'desolated,' surely, not 'squandered.'

44. 'Thy' is emphatic. There is a reminiscence (doubt-less unconscious) of CIX. 24.

SECTIONS I.-IV.

There is a distinct, though not very close, connection in these sections. The poet will not suppress his grief lest he should suppress love too (I.). This grief, however, in the phases de-scribed in II., III., IV. proves to be sullen, morbid, or weakening. He questions its worth (III.), and then rouses himself against it (IV.). It is not sorrow like this that must be cherished for the sake of love.

I.

'Loss may in the end be gain, but not if the gain be snatched at prematurely. To stifle sorrow at first would be to stifle love, and the final result would be the mere death of the old self, not its death into life.' A main idea of the poem, that love is the supreme good and can defy time, is expressed at once in the opening section.

1-4. Tennyson in his later years believed that he had alluded here to Goethe. He might easily have been familiar in youth with the famous lines in *Faust*, 'Entbehren sollst du,' etc., and during the thirties Carlyle was writing, in connection with Goethe, on the idea of 'self-annihilation,' more than once quoting the sentence, 'It is only with Renunciation that Life, properly speaking, can be said to begin' (see *e.g. Sartor*, II. ix.). With line 2 cf. Tennyson's remark to Prof. Sidgwick, 'Goethe is consummate in so many different styles' (*Memoir*, II. 392).

3, 4. For the metaphor Gatty compares St. Augustine, 'De vitiis nostris scalam nobis facimus, si vitia ipsa calcamus,' which suggested Longfellow's *Ladder of St. Augustine*, published in 1858. The image with Tennyson is that of a stair: cf. *Par. Lost*, v. 509-12 (Tainsh), VIII. 591, and lines from *The Princess* quoted on LV. 16. The use of 'stepping-stone' for 'step' seems to be very rare: the only other instance I know is in *Guy Mannering*, ch. LIII., where Meg Merrilies is the speaker. With 'dead selves' cf. *The Princess*, III., 'We touch on our dead self, nor shun to do it, Being other.'

7. Cf. *Tiresias*, 'Their examples reach a hand Far through all years.'

8. Cf. *Richard III*. IV. iv. 321 (G. A. C.):

> The liquid drops of tears that you have shed
> Shall come again, transformed to orient pearl,
> Advantaging their loan with interest
> Of ten times double gain of happiness.

Cf. also *Lucrece*, 1797, and Sonnets 31 and 74.

10. Cf. 'the raven down of darkness,' *Comus*, 251.

12. 'beat the ground': in dancing. Cf. CV. 17, and Horace's 'pulsanda tellus,' already translated in *Comus*, 143. There is an allusion, of course, to the Dance of Death.

13-16. The idea is that Time, years hence, having worn

away both the grief and the love of the poet, would boast of
his conquest, and laugh at the miserable outcome of so long
a love. With 'long result' cf. *Locksley Hall*, 'the long
result of time.' For the conquest of time by love cf. LXXXV.
65-8, CXXXI. 7, and in the *Memoir* (I. 307) a poem, originally
CXXVII. of *In Memoriam*, on the 'far-famed Victor Hours
That ride to death the griefs of men':

> Behold, ye cannot bring but good,
>> And see, ye dare not touch the truth,
>> Nor Sorrow beauteous in her youth,
> Nor Love that holds a constant mood.

II.

The poet sees in the yew-tree among the
graves an image, which fascinates him, of stubborn
absorption in the thought of death. Through a
thousand years, it seems to him, while flowers and
animals and men arose and perished, it has maintained its unchanging gloom, never blossoming or
even altering its hue.

He is abandoning himself to sorrow, though this
sorrow is at the opposite extreme to the intoxica-
tion described in the preceding section. The ideas
expressed are those of his sorrow, as in the next
section, and they come from a 'lying lip.' See
accordingly the second poem on the yew (XXXIX.).

4. Cf. Job, viii. 17: 'His roots are wrapped about the heap,
and he seeth the place of stones' (G. A. C.).

7. 'the clock' of the church-tower behind the yew. Cf.
Love and Death, and *The Two Voices*:

> I found him [death] when my years were few,
> A shadow on the graves I knew,
> And darkness in the village yew.

10. 'gale' seems to mean here a breeze in spring. This does not make the yew brighten in colour by flowering (5) or putting forth new shoots. 'Gale' without an adjective means in our older poetry simply a wind, not a strong wind; and such phrases as 'gentle gales' are common. Tennyson generally follows this use.

11, 12. Nor does the summer sun brand it so that its colour, at the end of summer, becomes burning or fiery (cf. XCIX. 12, CI. 4). This interpretation, which has been suggested to me, seems much better than my former one, that the summer sun does not darken the foliage.

13. 'thee, sullen': first ed.: 'the sullen.' Evidently a mere misprint.

14. I take 'for,' with Gatty, to mean ' with desire for,' as in such a phrase as 'sick for home.' The word might, of course, mean 'because of,' the 'stubborn hardihood' of the yew being regarded with horror ; and so, presumably, it is taken by Beeching, who understands this poem and the next to present the alternatives, suggested in the opening section, of stoicism and of yielding to sorrow. [Mr. Beeching now agrees with my interpretation.]

III.

His sick sorrow, as in II., distorts the truth, and he now hesitates to yield to it further.

Here first appears the doubt, so often mentioned later, whether the world is not the meaningless and transitory product of blind necessity.

1. 'fellowship': so in *Demeter*, 'a far-off friendship,' for 'friend.'

5. Cf. 'Planets and Suns run lawless thro' the sky,' *Essay on Man*, I. 252.

6. This line may be taken with 5 : 'the stars, instead of moving in ordered courses, run blindly across the sky, weaving a tangled web': or it may be taken (more probably)

by itself to signify that the meaning of things is dark to us, 'the eternal Heavens' being hidden by woven clouds. Cf. CXXII. 4, LXXII. 8.

7. 'waste places' of the universe, not merely of the earth. The idea seems to be that of the pain in the world.

8. 'dying': probably an inference from the nebular hypothesis, so often referred to by Tennyson. Cf. CXVIII. 4.

10. 'the music': first ed.: 'her music.'

11. 'my': everyone naturally takes this to refer to the poet, whereas the quotation-marks compel us to refer it to Sorrow. But doubtless their insertion was an error in punctuation, as is suggested by Mr. Beeching and Mr. Ferrall.

11, 12. 'hollow': Tennyson is very fond of this word; *e.g.* 'Hollow smile and frozen sneer,' *The Poet's Mind*. Cf. LXX. 4, LXXIII. 13, and Virgil's 'cava sub imagine formae,' *Aen.* VI. 293.

14, 15. 'natural good': so she seemed at first (section I.); but *this* sorrow seems rather born of diseased blood. With 'vice of blood' cf. LIV. 4; also *Othello*, I. iii. 123, 'I do confess the vices of my blood' (G. A. C.).

IV.

Asleep he is enslaved by the dull stunned sense of loss; waking he resolves to master it.

Later (*e.g.* LXVIII. LXX. LXXI.) he dreams of the dead: here he is aware only that his heart has been so paralysed by the loss of something familiar and dear that he wishes to die.

4 f. Cf. Aug. *Conf.* IV. 4, of the time after his friend's death: 'I became a great puzzle to myself, and asked my soul why she was so sad and why she so exceedingly disquieted me, but she knew not what to answer to me' (G. A. C.)

6. 'fail from thy desire': rather 'lose the power of desiring' than 'lose the object desired.' With 'fail from' (='die away from') cf. II. 15, LXXXIV. 36.

10. As the friendship did not begin in childhood, 'early years' may be intended to emphasise the confusion of the dreaming mind. But it is barely possible that the phrase is an oversight, marking a late date of composition.

11, 12. 'Water can be lowered in temperature below the freezing point, without solidifying ; but it expands at once into ice if disturbed ; and the suddenness of the expansion breaks [may break ?] the containing vessel' (Gatty). With the metaphor of tears freezing cf. XX. 11, 12, and Byron ('There's not a joy'), 'That heavy chill has frozen o'er the fountain of our tears.'

15. 'the will': cf. 2, and LXXXV. 37-40.

V.

The first of those sections which deal with the poet's verses and their relation to his grief (see p. 26). Here his poetry is regarded merely as an anodyne : contrast XXXVIII.

9. 'weeds': garments, as often in the older poets.

11, 12. Cf. *Hamlet*, I. ii. 85 :

> But I have that within which passeth show ;
> These but the trappings and the suits of woe.

VI.

That loss is common to the race does not make his own loss less bitter. Contrast the tone of XCIX. Even here, however, his mood softens as he describes the sorrows of others. A passage in Taylor's *Holy Dying*, quoted by Gatty, may have suggested the section. On its date cf. p. 15.

2. Cf. *Hamlet*, I. ii. 72 :

> Thou know'st 'tis common : all that lives must die.

7, 8. Collins compares Lucr. II. 578-80 :

> Nec nox ulla diem neque noctem aurora secuta est,
> Quae non audierit mixtos vagitibus aegris
> Ploratus.

15, 16. These magnificent lines are hardly injured by the reminiscence of *Richard III.*, I. iv. 37 :

> but still the envious flood
> Kept in my soul, and would not let it forth
> To seek the empty, vast and wandering air.

23, 24. The inverted commas were added late.

26. 'ranging': a favourite word with Tennyson, appearing often in his early poems, though not often in this sense. Cf. 'the bee would range her cells,' *Two Voices*.

41-4. Cf. the last four stanzas of LXXXV.

VII.

He visits his friend's house (see p. 3). Contrast with the utter desolation of this poem the less striking but scarcely less beautiful later section, CXIX.

4. Cf. *Break, break, break* :

> 'But O for the touch of a vanish'd hand.'

7. For the idea cf. *Maud*, II. iv. st. x. :

> And on my heavy eyelids
> My anguish hangs like shame.

(This section of *Maud* was, in its original form, written not later than 1834.) For the phrase see *Hamlet*, I. i. 148 :

> 'And then it started like a guilty thing.'

But see also Wordsworth's *Immortality* Ode, IX., and an article on Associated Reminiscences by A. B. Cook in the *Classical Review*, October, 1901.

9. 'far away,' in busier streets.

VIII.

This section, by its softer tone, helps to effect a transition to the group which follows. Like V. it refers to his poems, but these are now cherished for his friend's sake.

The first two stanzas, as Mr. Collins notices, may have been suggested by the *Lover's Journey* of Crabbe.

5. Cf. 'And flung a magic light on all her hills and groves,' Coleridge, *France.*

8. Cf. 'And Lycius' arms were empty of delight,' Keats, *Lamia.* With the absence of rhyme in 'light,' 'delight,' cf. XIV. 1, 4, 'report,' 'port'; XXXV. 5, 8, 'here,' 'hear'; XLI. 17, 20, 'moor,' 'more'; LI. 14, 15, 'hours,' 'ours.'

9. Cf. Aug. *Conf.* IV. 4 : 'My native country was a torture to me, and my father's house a wondrous unhappiness ; and whatever I had enjoyed with him, wanting him, turned into a frightful torture. Mine eyes sought him everywhere, but he was not granted them, and I hated all places because he was not in them' (G. A. C.).

12. 'where thou art not': see on XXII. 19.

21. Cf. C. 17, and the line quoted on VII. 4.

SECTIONS IX.-XVII.

These sections form a group, connected by reference to the ship that brings the body of the dead from 'the Italian shore' to England. It is probably not an accident that the number of stanzas in the sections is uniform.

In thinking of the ship, and of the burial which will follow its arrival, the poet finds relief from his absorption in the sense of loss. The peace and beauty of some of the descriptions, the freer play of fancy, and the much fuller expression of love—a love which is extended to the ship that carries the dead friend and to the earth that will receive him—give to this group a tone of sweetness and tenderness which contrasts with that of most of the preceding sections.

The group must be supposed to cover several weeks (XVII. 7).

IX.

For the date of this section see p. 14.

The final lines are the first expression of tenderness in the poem.

'With Section IX. should be compared Horace, Ode iii., lib. i., and Theocritus, Idyll vii. 53 *sqq.*, which plainly inspired it' (Collins). Perhaps 'so' (5), the comparative 'ruder,' and the use, not always happy, of 'ocean-plains,' 'remains,' 'favourable speed,' 'lead . . . his urn,' 'prosperous,' and 'perplex,' may be due to the associations of Latin poetry, though the last two words are common in Milton.

9. 'ruder' than the air which by day gave such a speed as ruffled the mirror'd mast : or possibly 'too rude,' like 'nobler' in LX. I. (so Beeching).

10. 'Phosphor' : the morning star. Cf. CXXI.

13. He goes back to the 'night' of line 9. 'Sphere': cf. *Enoch Arden*, 'Then the great stars that globed themselves in Heaven.' Cf. Virgil's 'magnum glomerantur in orbem.'

17 f. I cannot doubt that the words of Constance (*King John*. III. iv. 88) were echoing in Tennyson's mind. There

are indications in *In Memoriam* of other reminiscences of the same scene.

18. Repeated XVII. 20, where this group of poems ends.

20. This line becomes the occasion of LXXIX.

X.

5. 'bring'st': first ed. 'bringest,' which, though at once changed, reappeared in some editions.

9. 'So': gently and safely, as in IX. 5.

10. 'This look of quiet' in the ship as he imagines it. It is an 'idle dream' that this quiet can matter to the dead, a 'home-bred fancy' that makes us wish that the dead should 'rest' in earth and not be 'tossed' in the roaring sea ; but he yields to the dream and the fancy. Cf. XVIII. 5-8.

14. 'takes': a favourite word with Tennyson. Cf. XVI. 5.

15, 16. The chancel where the villagers receive the sacrament.

17. 'wells.' This word is used by Tennyson in peculiar ways. If the present passage stood alone, 'wells' might be due to a recollection of Scott's *Pirate*, ch. XXXVIII., 'The wells of Tuftiloe can wheel the stoutest vessel round and round'; where 'wells' means whirlpools in the sea, and probably represents an Orcadian word (see Jamieson, *s.v.*). Or if Tennyson knew the English dialectic 'weel' or 'weal,' an eddy, whirlpool, or pool, in a river, he might (wrongly) have supposed it to be the dialect form of the standard 'well.' But from the use of 'wells' in *The Princess*, V. :

> Or by denial flush her babbling wells
> With her own people's life ;

in *The Two Voices* :

> To-day I saw the dragon-fly
> Come from the wells where he did lie ;

in *Oenone* :

> Idalian Aphrodite, beautiful,
> Fresh as the foam, new-bathed in Paphian wells;

and in CVIII. 8, 'dive below the wells of Death,' it seems
most likely that, in all the passages under review, Tennyson
uses the standard 'wells' for waters that have issued from
a well-spring, whether of fresh water or of sea water (cf. 'the
fountains of the great deep,' *Gen.* VII. 11). I have to thank
Dr. J. A. H. Murray for information about standard 'well'
and the other word or words.

19. Cf. *The Princess*, VI. : 'hands so lately claspt with
yours.'

20. 'Tangle': sea-weed. Tennyson speaks of 'sea-tangle'
in a letter (*Memoir*, I. 173).

XI.

The spirit of calm and beauty which is breathed
by the two preceding sections culminates in this
exquisite poem. The time is the early morning of
an autumn day, the scene a Lincolnshire wold,
from which a great plain sweeps to the eastern
sea. The sight of the sea carries the poet's mind
to the Mediterranean, the ship, and its freight, by
a transition of wonderful dignity and pathos.

2. 'calmer' than mine (see 15, 16) ; or perhaps generally
'grown more calm.'

8. 'that twinkle into green and gold,' as the dew-drops on
them catch the sun.

11. The church-towers, a striking feature of Lincolnshire
landscapes, are mentioned again in XV. 7.

12. 'bounding': limiting, as in XVII. 6.

15, 16. With this uncertainty cf. his bewilderment at the
apparent change in his feelings (XVI.), and the dream-like
strangeness described in XIII. 13-20.

17. 'silver sleep': cf. Epilogue, 116.

20. Cf. Byron, *Bride of Abydos*, II. xxvi. : 'His head
heaves with the heaving billow' (G. A. C.).

XII.

The calm of the preceding poems gives place to a wild unrest, in which the poet's soul seems to leave his body and fly to meet the coming ship. The restless movement of the verse is in strong contrast with the rhythm of XI.

6. 'mortal ark.' Gatty seeks to explain this strange phrase by reference to ' our earthly house of this tabernacle' (2 Cor. V. 1), but the phrase appears again in *The Two Voices* in a context which shows that the poet imagined the ark as a vessel at sea ('Who sought'st to wreck my mortal ark'). Here at any rate it seems certain that the association of the dove and the ark in the story of the Flood suggested the phrase.

9. At each stage of the flight the sea appears below as a vast circular mirror. So in *Enoch Arden* the ship moves 'Thro' many a fair sea-circle day by day.' From the first Tennyson's poems show a special fondness for circular or spherical appearances in landscape : cf. IX. 13, XXIV. 15, 16, XXXIV. 5, LXXXVI. 5.

12. 'the marge': the horizon opposite to the point where the sails are seen rising. Cf. XLVI. 7, 16. It seems to be imagined as a kind of beach, and perhaps 'rounded' in 9 may mean convex as well as circular.

19. 'the body': the 'weight of nerves without a mind.'

XIII.

This section and the next describe the dreamy stupor of a mind exhausted by grief and unable to realise the loss which has stunned it. In such a mood fancy can flit around the ship, almost forgetful of the burden it carries.

1-4. The stanza is frequently misunderstood. It is taken to describe the widower's sudden and overwhelming realisation of his loss in the moment when, waking from sleep, he 'feels her place is empty,' and knows that he has only dreamed of her. But the fourth stanza shows that this is not so, and that *everything* described in the first stanza, the dream, the doubt, the movement, and the weeping, takes place in sleep, or, at any rate, before a full awakening. So the poet's consciousness of his loss has the strangeness and uncertainty of a dream, or of a state between sleeping and waking. The source of the difficulty lies in the second and third stanzas, which seem to express such a clear consciousness of the nature of his loss as would come to the widower when fully awake. [I am not sure that this interpretation is right. It is perhaps as probable that the usual understanding of the first lines is correct, and that there is some want of connection between the first three stanzas and the last two.]

3, 4. Cf. Aeschylus, *Ag.* 420 f.; Ovid, *Her.* x, 9 ff.; Pope, *Eloisa to Abelard*, 235 ff.

9-12. This stanza also is sometimes, and strangely, misunderstood. He weeps the comrade of his choice, now become an awful thought, a life removed ; he weeps the human-hearted man he loved, now become a Spirit. See Introduction, pp. 41, 42.

13. First ed. : 'Come Time, and teach me many years': whence 'many years' was construed as = 'during many years.'

16. For the idea, that at this stage of grief tears fall only when the full meaning of loss is not felt, cf. IV. 11, 12, XIX. 9 ff., XX. Contrast XLIX., a later stage. The idea in 'leisure' and 'time' (17) seems to be that, if he realised the truth, he would not yield to grief but would exert his will ; cf. LXXXV. 37-40.

19, 20. With the peculiar effect of these lines, due to the alliteration on *b* and the repetition of sharp final consonants cf. VII. 12.

XIV.

Addressed, like IX., X., XV., XVII., to the ship.

The last line, by recalling XIII. 15, strengthens the sense of connection. The poem is technically remarkable as forming a single sentence, like LXIV., LXXXVI., CXXIX., CXXXI.

XV.

This fine poem must be read in connection with its predecessors. The storm from the west at sunset contrasts with the windless calm of the sunny morning in XI. The half-delusive calm of spirit expressed in IX., X., XI. continues ; and therefore, in spite of the storm at home, the ship is still imagined as moving over a glassy sea. But something of the 'wild unrest' of XII. is also present, and it would sympathise with the storm but for fears that after all the ship too may be in tempest.

1. 'begin': first ed.: 'began.' The mixture of tenses remains in the next stanza, unless 'crack'd,' 'curl'd,' and 'huddled' are to be taken as participles.

2. 'dropping day': Virgil's 'Oceani finem juxta solemque cadentem,' *Aen.* IV. 480? Or Shakespeare's 'drooping west,' 2 *Hen. IV.*, Ind.?

3. Cf. XI. 3, 7, 14. The time is later.

'the last red leaf': cf. 'the one red leaf, the last of its clan,' *Christabel.*

7. 'tower': cf. XI. 11.

11. 'molten glass': Gollancz compares 'a molten looking-glass,' *Job* xxxvii. 18 (of the sky). Cf. 'the sea of glass,' *Rev.* xv. 2 (G. A. C.).

12, 13. For he would hear in fancy the straining masts and cordage of the ship in storm.

18. 'labouring': 'anticipated by Marlowe (*Dr. Faustus ad finem*):—Into the entrails of yon labouring cloud' (Collins). In that line the metaphor is from the 'labour' of child-birth, and so it is also, I suppose, in *l'Allegro*,

> Mountains on whose barren breast
> The lab'ring clouds do often rest;

but in the present passage 'labouring,' I think, means merely 'toiling,' as in *Hyperion*:

> As if the vanward clouds of evil days
> Had spent their malice, and the sullen rear
> Was with its stored thunder labouring up.

This seems almost certain if we compare the line,

> The vapour labours up the sky,

in the verses written soon after Hallam's death (*Memoir*, I. 107).

19. 'topples': threatens to fall from its height; as in *Alastor*, 'toppling stones.' Cf. the Wellington *Ode*, VIII. The word generally means to throw or fall from a height, as in CXXVII. 12.

20. Cf. Shelley, *Witch of Atlas*, XLVIII., 'the clouds whose moving turrets make The bastions of the storm' (G. A. C.).

XVI.

The alternation of calm despair and wild unrest expressed in the preceding poems bewilders the poet. Can his sorrow shift so quickly into varying forms? Or is it an abiding reality, untouched by these surface changes? Or is he so shaken by the shock of loss that his mind has become a mere stream of discordant and delirious images?

2. 'calm despair,' repeated from XI. 16; 'wild unrest,' repeated from XV. 15. The wild unrest is also seen in XII.

5. 'seem' is emphatic. The lake may reflect on its surface variations in the world above it, but its 'deep self' is always the same. 'Form' is often used by Tennyson for superficial appearance as contrasted with essential being. Another interpretation is given by C. E. Benham : 'Or is it simply that in sorrow man does not know his own state, but merely imagines that his surroundings represent his mood, while the real self is no more seen by the man than the lark's reflection is seen by the lake in which it is mirrored?'

12. It is the fear for the ship (XV. 14) that suggests this image, which again reminds the reader of the surrounding sections. Cf. Herbert's *Misery*, where man is compared with

> A sick toss'd vessel, dashing on each thing ;
> Nay, his own shelt.

17. As in XIV.

XVII.

This final section of the group refers back to the opening section, IX.

2. 'and my prayer,' etc., explains 'such a breeze,' etc.

6. Cf. XI. 12, XII. 9. Here the 'circle' is the circular horizon.

8. Apparently he goes back to the time of waiting, when he counted the weeks and days, and longed for the arrival of the ship. Mr. Benham, however, supposes that the ship has not yet quite arrived, and that the poet is expressing his present desire for its arrival. This is perhaps the more natural interpretation, if we suppose the ship to be signalled some days before it comes into port.

10. Cf. Moore, *How dear to me* : 'And as I watch the line of light that plays,' etc. (G. A. C.).

13. Cf. 'Sic fratres Helenae,' etc., in Horace's Ode referred to in IX.

15, 16. Cf. *Queen Mab*, 'Stars, your balmiest influence shed.' Cf. also *The Talking Oak*,

> All starry culmination drop
> Balm-dews to bathe thy feet!

and the *Lotos-Eaters* : Choric Song, i.

19, 20. See IX. 17, 18.

XVIII.

The Burial. The final stanzas are not only among the most pathetic in the poem, but mark clearly the advance from the blind sense of loss to a sorrow not less keen, but softened by the expression of love and mingled with resolution. Line 18 recalls the idea, which at first seemed almost vain,

> That men may rise on stepping-stones
> Of their dead selves to higher things.

As yet, however, the thought of 'a meeting somewhere friend with friend' is not entertained.

The section illustrates Tennyson's statement that *In Memoriam* does not profess to be strictly biographical. For the date of Hallam's burial, see pp. 3, 20 note. Further, he was buried in Clevedon Church, not in the churchyard, and Tennyson says that he did not see Clevedon till years afterwards.

1. G. A. C. compares with this and X. 11 ff. Ovid, *Trist.* I. ii. 53-6 :

> Est aliquid, fatove suo ferrove cadentem
> In solida moriens ponere corpus humo :
> Et mandare suis aliquid, sperare sepulcra,
> Et non aequoreis piscibus esse cibum.

3, 4. It seems likely, from the use of 'ashes,' and perhaps of 'blest' in line 6, that there is a reminiscence, not of *Hamlet* v. i. 262, but of Persius, *Sat.* I. 39, quoted by Collins,

> Nunc non e tumulo fortunataque favilla
> Nascentur violae?

5-8. Cf. X. 11 ff. and Introduction, p. 3.

11. 'whatever loves': the construction is an echo of XVII. 13.

14, 15. Cf. *2 Kings*, IV. 34 (G. A. C.).

XIX.

This lovely poem (an old friend of Tennyson's told me) was written in Tintern Abbey. The first five lines merely connect the Wye, to which the poet is listening, with the thought of his friend. The tidal water, in flowing up the Bristol Channel, which, as it begins to narrow, is called the Severn, passes Clevedon and, further up, enters the Wye. The main idea is expressed in the last three stanzas, and is quite clear, though it has been strangely misunderstood. As the tide passes up the Wye, its silent flood deepens and hushes the river; but as it ebbs again, the river, growing shallower, becomes vocal and 'babbles.' And so, when the tide of sorrow floods the poet's heart, he cannot sing or even weep; but when it ebbs his grief can find a voice.

Cf. *Rape of Lucrece*, 1328:

> 'Tis but a part of sorrow that we hear:
> Deep sounds make lesser noise than shallow fords,
> And sorrow ebbs, being blown with wind of words.

2. The association of darkness with death seems to have been very strong with Tennyson. Cf. 'If I make dark my countenance,' *Two Voices*; 'the dark dissolving human heart,' *Princess*, III.

7. 'half': *i.e.* the Wye is tidal for about half its course.

9. 'nor moved along': its natural course to the sea is arrested.

14. 'vocal': a favourite word with Milton.

XX.

This section, through a simile, more homely than that of its predecessor, describes the same difference between the 'deeper anguish' which is dumb, and the 'lesser griefs that may be said.'

12. Byron's use of this metaphor has been quoted on IV. A poem by Sara Coleridge has the lines,

> But tears will take the accustomed course
> Till time their fountains freeze.

17-20. This stanza seems to be an anti-climax which injures the poem. The children are, indeed, made to think of the past, while the servants can speak of the future ; but the thought, 'How good ! how kind ! and he is gone,' hardly answers to the description in the fine stanza which precedes, nor does it express a sorrow which the servants might not feel.

XXI.

The last two poems have implied that the mourner's songs express but little of his deeper grief. Still he defends them against imagined attacks. This is the third of the sections which deal with his poetry (cf. V. and VIII.).

The conventions of the classical pastoral elegy,

in which the singer is supposed to be a shepherd, are employed. They occur in *In Memoriam* only here and there, and perhaps generally with a jarring effect.

15, 16. Cf. for the collocation of these lines with the next stanza, the lines in *Locksley Hall* beginning, 'Eye to which all order festers.'

19, 20. 'and charms': 'Science every month is evolving some new secret' (Gatty). I take the words with the preceding clause: 'Science is making the most lately discovered moon disclose its nature'; 'moon' being either the same as 'world,' or else = 'satellite,' as distinguished from 'world.' Perhaps Gatty's interpretation is supported by the lines,

> Each month is various to present
> The world with some development

(*Two Voices*), and by the use of 'moons' in XXVI. 3, LXXVII. 8. The other is confirmed by XCVII. 22, and would be made certain by a passage in *Memoir*, II. 336, where Tennyson is described as saying 'that the spectroscope was destined to make much greater revelations even than it had already made, in charming "Her secret from the latest moon,"' if we were sure that the poet himself used the quotation. Mr. Jacobs thinks there is a reference to the discovery of Neptune, 'substantiated September, 1846' (and so takes 15, 16 to apply to the Chartist movement). This would give a very late date to the section, and of course it is not necessary to suppose that Tennyson refers to any one discovery ; but the phrase, 'to feel from world to world,' is beautifully appropriate to the process by which the existence of Neptune was guessed at from the irregularities in the motion of Uranus, and Mr. Eve remarks that two of the satellites of Uranus were rediscovered in 1847.

24. Cf.   Ich singe wie der Vogel singt,
                 Der in den Zweigen wohnet,

The Harper's Song in *Wilhelm Meisters Lehriahre*, II. xi.

25, 27. First ed. : 'And unto one her note.'

27. Cf. 'Sorrow hath changed its note,' Herbert, *Joseph's Coat.*

SECTIONS XXII.-XXV.

These sections form a distinct group, in which, for the first time, the poet looks back to the past and compares the present with it.

XXII.

Collins finds 'an exact counterpart' to this section in Petrarch's 47th Sonnet *In Morte di Madonna Laura*, of which there certainly seem to be reminiscences.

3. The path seems to be figured as ascending in spring and summer, and descending in autumn and winter. See 10 and 11.

6. 'crown'd': cf. LXXII. **5.** It is a favourite word in Shakespeare's Sonnets.

10. September 15 was the date of Hallam's death.

12. The image of Death as a shadow occurs frequently in Tennyson, as in writers before him : for instance, in the early poem, *Love and Death*, Death is described as the shadow cast by life in the light of eternity.

19. 'waste': the path has entered a desert. Cf. A. H. Hallam, *Remains*, p. 65 (G. A. C.) :

> Sick and lone,
> Roaming the weary desert of my doom,
> Where thou art not.

The last three lines, with the next section, seem to be the only allusion in *In Memoriam* to the longing for death which the poet felt for a time, and partly expressed in the *Two Voices*. (See *Memoir*, I. 109.)

XXIII.

1. Of course 'sometimes' does not qualify 'wander,' as in Gatty's paraphrase, but answers to 'Or.' 'Sometimes in dumb sorrow, sometimes breaking into a song of mourning.'

3. For the pathetic effect of the repetition, cf. XVIII. 13, and *Rape of Lucrece*, 795, 'where I alone alone must sit and pine.' David's cry for Absalom, Othello's 'But yet the pity of it, Iago! O Iago, the pity of it, Iago!' Lear's 'Thou'lt come no more, Never, never, never, never, never,' Hamlet's thrice-repeated 'Except my life,' are among famous examples of this effect.

4, 5. Death, himself a mystery, can alone disclose the mysteries concealed in the creeds. In the metaphor there may be a reminiscence of *Cymbeline*, V. iv. 7, 'death, who is the key To unbar these locks,' or of the golden key of *Comus*, 13, *Lycidas*, 110.

6. 'wander': he no longer 'walks in haste' to find the Shadow, but wanders without a purpose; 'lame': cf. LV. 17.

12. 'Pan': the god of universal nature.

15, 16. Cf. 'Ev'n thought meets thought ere from the lips it part,' Pope, *Eloisa to Abelard*, 95.

17, 18. 'met,' in the present; 'bring,' in the future.

21-4. The use of 'Pan' for 'Nature' in 12 might lead one to think that Tennyson is using the conventions of classical elegy, in which case the present stanza would refer to philosophy and poetry in general; but 'old' implies that he means Greek philosophy and poetry in particular. With 'divinely' cf. LIII. 14.

XXIV.

'But was the past really perfect? Does it not only seem so now?'

3, 4. Nothing is perfect. The sun itself has spots, dark moving islands in its sea of glory. Tennyson seems to have been fond of 'dash'd': cf. LII. 14, LXXXIII. 11

5. See XXIII. 17. This could not really be.

8. First ed. : 'Since Adam left his garden yet.' The change was not made till about 1878.

9-16. Two causes of the appearance of perfection in the past are suggested, not three : either contrast with the miserable present (stanza 3), or else the enchantment of distance which *always* attaches to the past, whatever the present may be (stanza 4).

10. First ed. : 'Hath stretch'd my former joy so great?' Cf. *Guinevere* :

> The moony vapour rolling round the King,
> Who seem'd the phantom of a Giant in it.

11, 12. The present is regarded as a low ground, in contrast with which the past stands out in high relief.

15, 16. From a distance the irregularities of the earth's surface and illumination would be lost to view, and it would appear a disc of 'glory.' (I owe the interpretation to Mr. Larden.) Cf. *Locksley Hall Sixty Years After* :

Hesper—Venus—were we native to that splendour or in Mars,

We should see the Globe we groan in, fairest of their evening stars.

So Landor, *Marvell and Parker*, 'The stars themselves are only bright by distance : go close and all is earthly' (G. A. C.).

XXV.

'The past was not perfect, but love removed all sense of its imperfection.'

1. 'Life': and therefore not perfect.

2. 'with equal feet': perhaps a reference to Virgil's 'sequiturque patrem non passibus aequis,' *Aen.* II. 724.

6. 'Possibly an intentional contrast with XII.' (Eve).

12. Cf. Bacon, Essay 27 : 'This communicating of a man's self to his friend . . . cutteth grief in halfes.'

SECTIONS XXVI.-XXVII.

The retrospect ends, but it has led the poet to recognise that Love outweighs whatever pain it may bring ; and, certain that it may endure even when its object is out of sight, he desires to live, and would not purchase happiness at the cost of Love.

XXVI.

2. Contrast XXII. and XXIII. His object in following the path is no longer to meet the Shadow, though he would desire to meet it at once if further life meant the decay of Love.

10. Cf. *Princess*, III. :

Let there be light, and there was light : 'tis so :
For was, and is, and will be, are but is ;
And all creation is one act at once,
The birth of light : but we that are not all,
As parts, can see but parts, now this, now that,
And live, perforce, from thought to thought, and make
One act a phantom of succession : thus
Our weakness somehow shapes the shadow, Time.

The idea is repeated in *The Ancient Sage*. It is to be found in many authors, *e.g.* Augustine's *Conf.* XIII. 44, IX. 24, and Browne's *Rel. Med.* I. 11 (G. A. C.). There is a curious coincidence of phrase in Marston's *Sophonisba*, II. ii., 'Gods naught foresee, but see, for to their eyes Naught is to come or past.'

12. 'See, in the Love that is, the indifference that will be.'

13. First ed. : 'So might I. . . .'

16. 'shroud': first ed., 'cloak'; 'proper scorn': self-scorn.

XXVII.

2, 3. Cf. 'Chill Penury represt their noble rage,' Gray's *Elegy*: also (G. A. C.) Scott's *Lady of the Lake*, VI. xxii.,

> The captive thrush may brook the cage,
> The prisoned eagle dies for rage.

5, 6. 'takes his license,' lives without law, because untroubled by promptings of a higher nature; 'field of time': earthly life; cf. XLIII. 14, XCI. 6. With this stanza cf. a remarkable extract from a letter, *Memoir*, I. 170.

11. Cf. *Hamlet*, I. iv. 32, but Tennyson's metaphor is of a stream clogged with weeds.

12. 'want': deficiency.

13-16. With this conviction the poem comes to a break, as though a definite stage of advance were reached; and the phrases 'I hold it true' and 'loved and lost' may be intended to indicate this by reminding the reader of I. 1, 15.

As a parallel to the last two lines (repeated LXXXV. 3, 4), Collins quotes Congreve, *Way oj the World*, II. ii.: ''Tis better to have been left than never to have been loved.' In the form of the expression there may be a reminiscence, certainly unconscious, of Campbell's *Jilted Nymph*:

> Better be courted and jilted
> Than never be courted at all.

SECTIONS XXVIII.-XXX.

What has been called in the Introduction the Second Part of *In Memoriam* begins here (see p. 31).

So far the poet's thoughts have been concentrated on his grief and love, and on the past. The idea of the continued life of the beloved dead now emerges, and in various forms becomes the principal subject of this Second Part. It is introduced at the close of this group of three sections referring to the first Christmas-tide after the death of the poet's friend.

XXVIII.

For the date of composition, see p. 14.

7. 'Swell out and fail,' as the wind (9) rises and falls, for mere changes in loudness would hardly produce the effect so well described in the next words.

8-12. I understand that each of the four churches has four bells (5, 9, and CIV.), and that these four bells seem to be ringing 'peace and goodwill,' and then 'goodwill and peace,' and then 'peace and goodwill,' and then 'to all mankind.' Each syllable, that is, in lines 11, 12 represents the sound of a bell. For a suggestion as to the possible churches see Rawnsley, *Memories of the Tennysons*, p. 12.

13. 'This year.' The expression suggests at first that the occasion is the second Christmas after the death of his friend. But see XXX. 15, 16.

18. He is at his father's house, where his childhood was spent.

XXIX.

2. 'household peace': *our* 'household peace'; not 'for death is ever invading some home.' The phrase occurs in *Par. Lost*, X. 908.

9. 'Yet go': he addresses members of the household who are going to decorate the church.

11. 'Use and Wont': Gatty aptly quotes the motto to the *Pirate*, ch. XIV.

16. Cf. CV.

XXX.

The Christmas-eve which had been anticipated and had begun in sadness, ends in cheerfulness and hope. Suddenly, and in tones of triumphant confidence, there are introduced the ideas of the continued and higher existence of the dead, and of their continued love for the living. For the date of this section, see p. 14.

8. 'one mute Shadow': surely the dead friend, not Death. Contrast the Epilogue, 85-88. See Introduction, pp. 41-43.

13. 'echo-like': explained by the next lines.

14, 15. The poet audaciously, for the sake of the sound, uses the two forms 'sung' and 'sang' in successive lines.

16. See p. 20.

25-28. 'The soul, freed from instability and weakness, unchanged in essence, but with strengthened powers, passes from embodiment to embodiment upon world after world.'

'seraphic flame': cf. Milton's 'flaming seraph' (*P.L.*, v. 875), and 'bright seraphim in burning row' (*At a Solemn Music*). For the collocation of 'rapt' with 'seraphic flame' cf. Pope's 'rapt seraph that adores and burns,' *Essay on Man*, I. 278. Cf. XLI. 1-4.

'veil.' Cf. *Sir John Oldcastle*, 'He veil'd Himself in flesh.'

The idea that the soul passes through life after life appears elsewhere in Tennyson (*e.g.* in the *Two Voices* and in *De Profundis*). Here we have the additional ideas that in each life it is embodied, and that the successive embodiments are on different worlds. Cf. LXXXII. 5, 6, LXXIII. I,

> So many worlds, so much to do,

and in *The Ring* the lines which Tennyson 'would quote as giving his own belief that "the after-life is one of progress"' (*Memoir*, II. 365):

> No sudden heaven, nor sudden hell, for man,
> But thro' the Will of One who knows and rules—

> And utter knowledge is but utter love—
> Æonian Evolution, swift or slow,
> Thro' all the Spheres—an ever opening height,
> An ever lessening earth.

In *In Memoriam*, the poet is content at last to leave these matters undefined.

32. 'Hope': the hope of immortality, born with Christ? 'He said to Bishop Lightfoot: "The cardinal point of Christianity is the Life after Death" {2 Tim., ch. I.).' *Memoir*, I. 321.

SECTIONS XXXI.-XXXVI.

The connection of these sections may be shown by the following analysis, which has no other purpose. The poet finds ' revealed ' in the story of Lazarus the fact of a life beyond death, but only the fact (XXXI.). He thinks that in the mind of Lazarus' sister curiosity as to the state beyond death was absorbed in love and adoration ; and in this attitude he finds a blessedness less securely attained by minds whose faith in immortality rests solely on inward evidence (XXXII., XXXIII.). It is true that such a faith is not only possible but seems forced on us by the inward evidence (XXXIV., XXXV.) ; but he is thankful for the sanction given to it by the revelation of Christ's life and teaching (XXXVI.).

XXXI.

' What has been revealed of the state after death ? The story of Lazarus tells us that he was raised again, but tells us nothing more.'

The transition to this section from the last

three stanzas of XXX. is surely obvious and natural. It has been considered strange that the poet, turning to the Gospel story, should think of the resurrection of Lazarus, not that of Christ; but he writes as a believer who is wondering what happens to a merely human soul after death. Cf. with this section and the next, Browne, *Religio Medici*, I. 21, 'I can read . . . that Lazarus was raised from the dead, yet not demand where, in the interim, his soul awaited.'

For the date of the section see p. 14.

3, 4. Did he lose his 'mortal sympathy' (XXX. 23)? 'To hear': at hearing.

6. The *Palace of Art* has a similar line :

There comes no murmur of reply.

8. 'added praise to praise': doubled our gratitude ; we are told that death is not extinction, but not what death is.

14. Pope's lines, *Eloisa to Abelard*, 9, 10,

Dear fatal name! rest ever unreveal'd,
Nor pass these lips in holy silence seal'd,

evidently remained in Tennyson's memory.

15, 16. 'He': Lazarus: 'that Evangelist': St. John, in whose Gospel alone the story is told.

XXXII.

' Perhaps Mary did not ask that question, *Where wert thou, brother, those four days ?* Curiosity as to the life after death was absorbed in joy, prayer, and love. And is not this the purest and most blessed state of mind ? '

In this state of mind is to be noticed not only the supersession of ' subtle thought ' and ' curious fears' by higher feelings, but also the absorption and endurance of love for a brother in a higher love (l. 14). This idea of love for the dead passing into and enduring in a higher love appears here first in *In Memoriam*, and anticipates the latest sections of the poem (see CXXIX., CXXX., and Prologue).

1. 'prayer': the word here, and in 13 and XXXIII. 5, seems to mean 'adoration.'

3, 4. 'Except the thought "He was dead,"' etc.

5. 'supersede': the poet's thought is more fully expressed by 14.

8. Cf. *John*, xi. 25, 'Jesus said unto her, I am the resurrection and the life' (G. A. C.).

15. 'so pure': so pure as these.

XXXIII.

This section is connected with its predecessor in so far as the state of mind of the 'sister' bears some resemblance to that attributed to Mary in XXXII. In the brother a different attitude is described. From the toil and storm of thought and doubt he has reached what seems to him a purer air. His faith is not attached to any event or person serving as a centre or type; it can find a centre in anything, and needs no image of a lawgiver to enforce the authority of the law within. He is warned not to disturb his sister's simpler faith, which is not less pure, and issues in a life happier and more actively good than his own.

The poet's meaning has been perverted by commentators. The brother addressed in XXXIII.

is apparently not a believer in 'truth revealed'; but it is quite a mistake to describe him as 'a sceptic' (Gatty), or as holding a 'vague form of scepticism' (Palgrave). He holds a 'faith' (3, 9); and in particular he is evidently supposed to believe in the 'divine truth' of immortality, otherwise the appeal of 11, 12 would have no force for him. It is also incorrect to say that the brother's faith is condemned as less true than the sister's. The question of truth is not raised. What the poet dwells on is the purity, blessedness, and active goodness connected with the sister's belief, and less securely connected with an intellectual faith like the brother's.

On the other hand we must reject the plausible idea that Tennyson is thinking of himself and his sister, so that the poem is addressed to himself; for in sections XXXI., XXXII., XXXVI., XXXVII. the poet certainly speaks as a believer in 'truth revealed.' He may, of course, be describing a mind of the same type as his own. With this section cf. XCVI.

3, 4. For the antithesis of 'faith' and 'form' cf. CXXVII. 1, and *Akbar's Dream*, where the thought of XXXVI. is also repeated.

6. 'Her early Heaven': 'the Heaven of which she was taught in childhood' (cf. XCVII. 30), not, I think, 'the Heaven n which she already dwells,' as may be suggested by Pope, *Eloisa to Abelard*, 300, 'And Faith, our early immortality.'

'views': prospects, that on which she gazes.

9. 'pure': see 2.

16. 'such a type' as 'the flesh and blood' of Christ (11).

H

XXXIV.

In this section and in XXXV. the poet turns from 'truth revealed' to seek for intimations of immortality in his own nature (such intimations as might be sought by the brother of XXXIII.). The world would have no meaning for him, life no value for him, God no claim on him, if man were not immortal (XXXIV.). It is vain to reply that even then Love might give a value to life; for Love would wither under the knowledge of its own mortality, just as it never would have come into being had man possessed such knowledge (XXXV.).

Such is the obvious purport of the two sections; but there appears to have been more than this in the poet's mind. For, if this is all, his 'own dim life' evidently does not show that life *is* immortal; it shows at most that unless life were *believed* to be immortal, that which is of most value in it would not have come into existence or continue to exist. Yet XXXVI., stanza I (which corresponds with XXXIV. I, 2), seems to say that the *fact* of immortality is implied in human life; for the truth made 'current coin' by Christ must surely be the truth that man *is* immortal, not the truth that a belief in his own immortality is required for his highest life. And, in the same way, according to the first stanza of XXXIV., as naturally construed, the poet's 'own dim life' is to teach him 'that life shall live for evermore,' not merely that, apart from a belief in immortality, the world would be meaningless and life worthless to him.

Perhaps what was in the poet's mind was the idea that certain things in man's nature imply his immortality (not merely his belief in it), because they would be inexplicable if he were merely mortal. His love, in the best sense, is one such thing: in the *Two Voices*, where this line of argument is suggested, others are indicated. In that case the truth of immortality might naturally be said to be 'deep-seated in man's mystic frame,' or implied in his 'dim life.' (Compare Introduction, pp. 57 ff.)

With these two sections compare the magnificent rhetoric of *Vastness* in the *Demeter* volume.

1. 'dim' probably answers to 'darkly' in XXXVI. 1; or 'dim life' may possibly mean, 'the very feebleness of my darkened life'; or 'dim' may possibly mean, 'dim, but still not utterly dark.'

5. The earth as it appears to inhabitants, and as it would appear from a distance: or (more probably) the earth and the sun, 'the flame that measures time,' Hymn in *Akbar's Dream*; cf. LXXII. 13.

9. The God of such a world would not be reason or goodness or love, and could have no claim on a being with spiritual wants (cf. CXX.). Or, if 'dim' in 1 be taken to mean 'feeble,' 'such as I' may be taken to mean 'so miserable as I.' Or 'such as I' may mean, 'a being placed in a dying world, and himself doomed to extinction.' I prefer the first interpretation.

XXXV.

8-12. Nature would appear to be merely an interminable process of meaningless change and unrest, in which the soul too was involved. With 10-12 cf. CXXIII.

9. Cf. *Alastor*, 'The thunder and the hiss of homeless streams.'

11. Cf. CXXIII. 5 ff. 'Æonian': hills that have lasted whole æons (CXXVII. 16) or ages. The context suggests that Tennyson derived this favourite word from works on geology.

14. 'forgetful shore': the shore of Lethe that brings forgetfulness. Cf. XCVIII. 8. For the use of 'forgetful' Collins quotes *Par. Lost*, II. 73, 'the sleepy drench Of that forgetful lake.'

19. 'as Death': as mere death or extinction. For the thought of these lines cf. Wordsworth on Epitaphs, and *Locksley Hall Sixty Years After*:

Gone for ever! Ever? no—for since our dying race began,
Ever, ever, and for ever was the leading light of man.
Those that in barbarian burials kill'd the slave, and slew the
    wife,
Felt within themselves the sacred passion of the second life.

24. 'batten'd': fed grossly, as in *Hamlet*, III. iv. 67. In *Lycidas*, 29, the verb is transitive.

XXXVI.

He returns to the train of thought in XXXII. and XXXIII. Though spiritual truths, such as that of immortality, are implied in human nature, we owe thanks none the less to Him who opened them to all and embodied them in His life.

1. 'manhood': human nature; 'join': meet; 'darkly': obscurely, so that they are only dimly visible. Cf. XXXIV. 1, and *Two Voices*:

> Ah sure within him and without,
> Could his dark wisdom find it out,
> There must be answer to his doubt.

2. 'mystic frame': cf. LXXVIII. 18.

5 ff. Wisdom, or the Word, adapted itself to merely human minds—minds which can receive, embodied in a tale, truths which, expressed in closely knit reasonings, would find no entrance. (The reference is not merely to the one truth of immortality.)

The 'tale' here is the Gospel narrative in general, not merely stories such as the Parables. For 'the creed of creeds' (see next stanza) seems to be the life which Christ lived, and so the record of that life with the truths embodied in it. For the emphasis on 'deeds' (cf. 'hands' in 10) cf. XXXII. 13, XXXIII. 10.

With the thought cf. *Akbar's Dream*, where religious 'Forms' are described as

> A silken cord let down from Paradise,
> When fine Philosophies would fail, to draw
> The crowd from wallowing in the mire of earth,
> And all the more, when these behold their Lord,
> Who shaped the forms, obey them, and himself
> Here on this bank in *some* way live the life
> Beyond the bridge.

Here the last lines repeat the idea of stanza 3.

9. 'the Word': the *Memoir* (I. 312) says that Tennyson explained that 'the Word' in this section 'was " the Word" as used by St. John, the Revelation of the Eternal Thought of the Universe.'

15, 16. Savages of the Pacific Islands.

XXXVII.

He closes the group by excusing himself for touching on 'truth revealed.'

1. The conception of Urania, generally the Muse of Astronomy, as the goddess of heavenly poetry, is Miltonic. Cf. the famous address in *Par. Lost*, VII. 1-20.

6. 'Parnassus': a hill (8) sacred to Apollo and the Muses. The laurel grows freely on its slopes. Poets were crowned with laurel.

9. Melpomene, the muse of Tragedy, here of Elegy. So in Spenser's *Shepherd's Calendar, November*.

11. 'ev'n': first ed. : 'but,' which word occurs in 13.

12. 'prevailing' almost = 'superior.'

15, 16. Cf. V. VIII. XXI.

19. First ed. : 'And dear as sacramental wine.'

21. He returns to the image of the path, XXII. ff.

23. 'master': surely not Christ, but 'the dear one dead. For see 18, and for 'master' cf. LXXXVII. 29.

XXXVIII.

This section and the next, both spring poems, intervene between the group just ended and that which begins at XL. The present section deals again with his songs.

2. 'alter'd': from what they were before he walked alone.

3. Cf. *The Princess*, VI. : ' No purple in the distance.'

5. Contrast the tone of LXXXIII., the poem of the next spring. The 'blowing season' is, of course, the season when flowers blow.

9 foll. This idea appears here for the first time in the sections about his poems. The certainty of XXX. that the dead do not 'lose their mortal sympathy' or 'change to us' has passed with the exaltation of the moment, and so the gleam of solace is 'doubtful' (8).

11. 'free': cf. LXXXV. 86.

XXXIX.

This section was written in April, 1868 (*Memoir*, II. 53), and appeared first in 1870.[1] It is addressed to the church-yard yew-tree, and refers to II., from which the words 'graspest at the stones' and 'the dreamless head' are repeated, and also to III., from which 'lying lips' comes. In II. the yew was said to preserve an unchanging gloom. Here the poet acknowledges that this was a falsehood of Sorrow's; for in spring the gloom of the yew is 'kindled at the tips.' 'Yes,' answers Sorrow, 'but it passes back into gloom.'

2 ff. At a particular stage of its flowering, a yew which bears male flowers, if struck, or even if shaken strongly by the wind, will send up the pollen (hence 'fruitful,' 'living') in a 'cloud' of yellow 'smoke.' The sight is sometimes almost startling, and Tennyson refers to it again in the *Holy Grail*:

Beneath a world-old yew-tree, darkening half
The cloisters, on a gustful April morn
That puff'd the swaying branches into smoke.

5. The change of feeling since section II. is beautifully shown by the contrast between this line and 'Thy fibres net the dreamless head' (II. 3).

6. 'golden hour' of spring: cf. LXXXV. 106.

7. The yew sometimes has male and female flowers on the same tree.

8-12. The poet interrupts his apostrophe with the words

[1] [Mr. Eve remarks that the section contains internal evidence of its late date, the action described in line 2 being scarcely credible in the poet who is supposed to have addressed the yew only a few months before in the language of section II.]

(to paraphrase very prosaically) : ' So I say ; but what is that I hear Sorrow whispering in reply? She whispers, "Yes, the gloom is lightened, but it soon returns."' That is, lines 1-7 refute Sorrow's falsehood (section II.) about the yew ; and lines 11, 12 give her answer to this refutation. The answer is in harmony with the mood of XXXVIII., but the poet can recognise that it, like her former whisper, is false ; *i.e.* that the interpretation she puts upon the fact is due to the same sickness that distorted nature in II. and III.

It is of course possible to take 8-10 as referring to section II., and 11, 12 as the poet's answer to 8-10 : ' But Sorrow said you did not change in spring. That was false, then ; your gloom *is* lightened, though only for a little while.' But I cannot believe that this interpretation is right. Mr. Robinson objects to the other because it requires 'whispers' and not 'whisper'd,' and because there are no inverted commas round the last two lines. But Tennyson's use of these commas, as of other punctuation-marks, was very erratic ; *e.g.* in VI. 23, 24, and CII. 9, 12, they were absent till about 1878, and they are so still in IV. 5, 12, XCIV. 8. And, as to 'whisper'd,' see LII. 6, LXXXIV. 45. A man who, while he is speaking, hears some one whispering an objection, may check himself and say, ' What was that you whispered? just as well as ' What is that you are whispering ?'

11, 12. The kindling at the tips is taken by Miss Chapman to refer to 'the tender green shoots,' by Gatty (if I understand him) to the flowers. In favour of the first view it may be said (1) that 'tips' is not very appropriate to the position of the flower of the yew ; (2) that in II. 11, 12 (if not in 10) there is a reference to the colour of the foliage ; and (3) that there appears here to be a reminiscence of Shelley, *Triumph of Life* :

> In the April prime,
> When all the forest tips began to burn
> With kindling green.

The language is certainly curiously similar, but even if there is a reminiscence, the associated 'tips' and 'kindling' might easily recur without the further idea of leaves. And in favour of Gatty's view (which is, I believe, that taken by the great majority of readers) it may be observed (1) that the point which Sorrow has to meet concerns the flower, and (2) that Miss Chapman's interpretation implies that the new shoots are already conspicuous while the yew is in bloom. This is not the fact, and Tennyson would hardly make a mistake in the matter when he had just been watching the 'smoking' of the yew. The slight inappropriateness of 'tips,' as applied to the flowers, is not of much moment.

SECTIONS XL.-XLVII.

In this group the poet returns to the subject suggested in XXXI. foll., of the state of the soul after death. In all his fancies or speculations the underlying question is that of the possibility of his ultimate reunion with his friend.

XL.

'If only the departure of the soul at death were wholly like the separation of a bride from her old home! But she can return or send tidings of her new and wider life, and the soul cannot.' Cf. LXXXII., and for the simile the lines *To H.R.H. Princess Beatrice*,

> The Mother weeps
> At that white funeral of the single life,
> Her maiden daughter's marriage.

1. 'widow'd' : cf. IX. 18, and elsewhere.

8. Collins compares : 'The April's in her eyes,' *Antony and Cleopatra*, III. ii. 43.

19. 'In those great offices that suit': until about 1883 the line read 'In such great offices as suit.' 'I hate that,' said the author, alluding to the juxtaposition of sibilants in 'as suit' (*Nineteenth Cent.*, Jan. 1893).

21. The effect of the line is like that of 'Ay me! I fondly dream!' in *Lycidas*, 56.

32. 'undiscover'd': cf. 'the undiscovered country,' *Hamlet*, III. i. 79.

XLI.

'And in the new life my friend may advance, through changes unshared and unwitnessed by me, so far that, although after death I go through the same changes, I shall never overtake him.'

The idea is suggested by XL., stanza 5. That the fear is not deeply-seated, but a fancy dim (XLII. 1), is indicated by the fine stanza, 'Yet oft' —an instance of what is comparatively rare in Tennyson, effect produced by abstention from description.

Cf. Bulwer, *Zanoni* (1842): 'For her and thee will there be even a joint hereafter? Through what grades and heavens of spiritualised being will her soul have passed, when thou, the solitary loiterer, comest from the vapours of the earth to the gates of light?' (G. A. C.). See p. 17.

5 f. The friend, no doubt, is still rising from high to higher, but the poet can no longer see how one stage leads to another.

'something strange': cf. *Tempest*, 'something rich and strange,' and CXXIX., 9.

9. 'Deep folly': *i.e.* the wish he is just going to utter.

11. 'the grades' which his friend has traversed since death.

12. 'flash': cf. XCV. 36.

13, 14. 'Men fear Death as children fear to go in the dark': Bacon, *Essay* II.

15, 16. 'And as that natural fear in children is increased with tales, so is the other' (*ib.*). These two lines must refer to the horrors of the world below imagined in Classical and Christian Mythology, and described by Dante and (with reserve) by Virgil. The word 'fields' is probably due to recollections of Virgil (*e.g.* 'lugentes campi,' *Aen.* vi. 441), and 'gulfs' possibly to the lines about Tartarus (*ib.* 577 f.). 'Howlings' is probably a reminiscence of Claudio's speech (*Measure for Measure*, III. i. 126),

> or to be worse than worst
> Of those that lawless and incertain thoughts
> Imagine howling :

or of *Hamlet*, v. i. 264,

> A ministering angel shall my sister be
> When thou liest howling.

'Forgotten' no commentator attempts to explain. It sounds like a reminiscence, but I do not know of what. 'Forgotten by Heaven' is the only meaning that seems probable. Cf. the lines from the Dedication of the *Palace of Art* (where note 'howling'),

> And he that shuts Love out, in turn shall be
> Shut out from Love, and on her threshold lie
> Howling in outer darkness.

[It has been suggested that 'forgotten' implies that stories of infernal horror have almost faded from his mind.] With the whole stanza cf. Browne, *Rel. Med.* I. 51, 52 (G. A. C.).

23. 'secular to-be': age-long future. Cf. LXXVI. 6, and 'a secular bird, ages of lives,' *Samson Agonistes*, 1711.

XLII.

'My fear was vain. On earth, though unequal, we were united by place and love ; and so, though unequal, we may be elsewhere.'

2. 'still' : always.
5. 'retain' : keep together.

XLIII.

'But perhaps my friend is not advancing now ; perhaps after death souls sleep till some general awakening. This would not separate us ; for when he awoke unchanged, his love would awake too.'

So far the poet has assumed that his friend immediately after death entered on a new conscious life ; and he has asked whether this new life has carried him so far away that the poet, at his own death, will be unable to rejoin him. Now he considers the possibility of an intermediate state of sleep, and the bearing of this possibility on the question of future communion. If, he says, this sleep is complete, so that no new experience comes to the soul, its memory and love will revive unchanged at the general awakening, when the friends will be together.

It is observable that in Tennyson's abstract of this section (*Memoir*, II. 421) the notion of a general re-awakening disappears. Indeed the whole thought of the section was foreign to his habitual mode of imagining the state after death. See pp. 52, 53.

2. The soul is compared with a flower which closes during the night.

5. 'Bare of the body,' and so suffering no change, and acquiring no new quality, through it.

7, 8. Its character is due solely to its earthly experience.

10. 'So': first ed.: 'But.' The phrase 'still garden' occurs also in *The Gardener's Daughter*.

11, 12. 'figured': marked with character-traces; 'enrolls': includes. The idea is that all the souls that ever lived on earth sleep, with all their experience enclosed in them, till a general re-awakening. I take 'figured leaf' to repeat the idea of 7, 8, 'leaf' meaning 'petal,' and 'figured' referring to its coloured markings or pattern. For 'leaf' cf. Shelley's lines,

> Rose-leaves, when the rose is dead,
> Are heaped for the beloved's bed ;

and *The Princess*, v.,

> But pure as lines of green that streak the white
> Of the first snowdrop's inner leaves.

The word 'figured' may be due to *Lycidas*, 105. Cf. LXI. 6.

No doubt the reference *may* be to the calyx-leaves which in some plants close round the flower (as Mr. Larden suggests), or even to a leaf like the spatha of an arum. If so, I should still understand 'figured' of surface-markings, not of the shape of the outline. But I feel no doubt that the *new* idea which enters with these lines is to be found in 'garden' and 'total world,' not in 'figured leaf.'

13. 'will': first ed.: 'would.'

14. 'in Time': in the earthly life. Cf. XXVII. 6 ; XCI. 6.

15. 'prime': daybreak (see 2).

XLIV.

This section suggests an alternative to the supposition of XLIII. 'Perhaps at death the soul does not fall asleep, but begins at once a new conscious life. And perhaps in that life its earthly experience is forgotten. Yet, even so, dim hints of that experience may come to it. If such a dreamy intimation should reach my friend, let it be to him the germ from which a complete recollection may arise.'

The general meaning of the section is quite clear, but the first stanza is extremely obscure, and the interpretation of the second and third depends on that of the first. I believe it is impossible to arrive at certainty about the meaning of these stanzas ; but I will attempt to set out the possible ways of taking them, dividing the interpretations into two main classes, according to the sense attached to the word ' he ' in line 3. This may mean either (*A*) ' the happy dead,' or (*B*) a man on earth.

A. ' He ' in line 3 is ' the happy dead ' of line 1. Ignoring for the moment line 2, we may state the meaning according to this view as follows : ' The dead man, in his new life, forgets the days before God shut him off from further experience through the senses, *i.e.* the years before his death (stanza 1). Yet, in spite of this, perhaps there may come to him in his new life an occasional intimation of those earthly days (stanza 2). And, if this happens, perhaps it may happen to *thee* (stanza 3).' The second and third stanzas refer to the same possibility, which is regarded generally in st. 2, and in particular reference to the poet's friend in st. 3.

How now is line 2 to be construed? In one of two ways. (*a*) As referring to a man on earth. ' Here on earth a man grows continuously, remembering at each step the steps already taken; but the dead man forgets the time before his death.' This interpretation seems to me almost impossible. Surely it is practically certain that ' the man ' of line 2, and ' he ' of line 3, are one and the same man. If they were not, Tennyson would at any rate have italicised ' he.'

(*b*) It is just possible to construe thus : ' Here on the earth we imagine the happy dead to be growing continuously (and remembering his earthly life); but in fact he has forgotten it.' ' The man ' and ' he ' are here the same person, and the contrast is between our imagination and the fact about him. But this interpretation also seems to me in the highest degree improbable.

View *A*, then, according to which ' he ' in line 3 is the dead man, appears to admit of no plausible interpretation of the first stanza, and therefore must be rejected.[1] Its one attraction is that it allows us to construe the extraordinary phrase ' God shut the doorways of his head ' in the easiest way. These ' doorways ' will be the organs of sense, through which impressions from without may be imagined entering and reporting themselves to the soul : death shuts them, and so

[1] Surely, also, lines 3 and 4 read like the statement of a known fact, not like the expression of a mere guess.

excludes the soul from any further experience of earthly objects.

B. ' The man ' of line 2, and ' he ' of line 3, are the same, viz., a man on earth. The 'he' of line 7 is the same man ; and stanza 2 refers to experience in the earthly life, while stanza 3 refers to experience in a life beyond death. The general interpretation will be as follows : ' In order to guess at the experience of the happy dead let us observe what happens to a man on earth. He forgets what happened to him in " the days before God shut the doorways of his head," and yet at times has strange feelings which, although he does not know it, are due to the experience of those days. In like manner, if death brings forgetfulness of the earthly life, the happy dead may yet have strange feelings which are really due to the earthly experience.'

What now are 'the days before,' etc., and ' the days ' of stanza 2 ? Several views are possible. Is Tennyson referring (*a*) to infancy, or (*b*) to a life before the earthly life, or (*c*) to both ?

(*a*) I will first give my own view and some reasons for it. Lines 3 and 4 refer to the months of infancy [1] before the closing of the sutures of the

[1][There would be no objection in *principle* to including the months of life in the womb, and in the Epilogue (123 ff.) Tennyson imagines the soul-life to begin at the moment of conception. But I see no sign that in XLIV. and XLV. he thought of any time except that between birth (cf. XLV. I, 16) and the emergence of self-consciousness and ' clear memory,' roughly dated at the closing of the sutures.]

skull, a change which generally takes place at some time in the second year after birth (this interpretation I owe to Gatty). The argument (here I am in disagreement with Gatty) will then be as follows : As a man forgets the experience of his infancy, yet in mature life has strange feelings really due to it, so the dead man in his second life may forget his first, and yet be obscurely reminded of it. There is, on this view, no allusion in the whole section to ' pre-existence,' *i.e.* an individual life prior to the earthly life.

In favour of this view these reasons may be given :

(1) There is nothing in the section inconsistent with it, and nothing which it fails to explain naturally.

(2) In *The Two Voices* reference is again made to the fact of our forgetting our infancy (the fact being there used in an argument for pre-existence) :

> Or if thro' lower lives I came,
> I might forget my weaker lot ;
> For is not our first year forgot ?
> The haunts of memory echo not.

(3) In *The Ring* two lovers are described as

> dead so long, gone up so far,
> That now their ever-rising life has dwarf'd
> Or lost the moment of their past on earth,
> As we forget our wail at being born.

(4) In the *Memoir* (II. 382) Lord Tennyson tells us : ' my father enjoyed the tree for the cottagers'

I

children, saying to my wife about her baby :
" Perhaps your babe will remember all these lights
and this splendour in future days as if it were a
memory of another life." ' This is exactly the
idea of the present section turned round.

(5) As to the ' doorways,' the reference to an
anatomical fact, and the use of an elaborate
periphrasis, are both highly characteristic of
Tennyson, and could easily be paralleled.

(*b*) It is possible, though I have not met with
the view, to take lines 2-8 to refer to pre-existence.
The argument will be : Here on earth a man
grows, but forgets the life that preceded this ; and
yet at times he has experiences which are really
reminiscences of it : and so, in the life that
follows his earthly one, he may have forgotten
it and yet have experiences which are really
reminiscences of it. ' The days before,' etc., will
be the days before his first death, *i.e.* the death
that closed his pre-earthly life, in which he was,
as on earth, body as well as soul, and had a head
with sense-organs in it.

In favour of this view it may be said that the
idea of pre-existence is not infrequent in Tennyson, and is prominent in *The Two Voices*, a poem
written not long after Hallam's death. Further,
in that poem (see the thirteen stanzas beginning
' It may be that no life is found ') there are
striking allusions to the phenomenon, mentioned
here, of ' mystic hints ' and ' touches,' considered
there as due to the forgotten experience of a

previous life. These again would be equivalent to the intimations of Wordsworth's Ode, which might have suggested this poem. Perhaps also the interpretation of the 'doorways'[1] is no stranger than Gatty's, while the fact that Tennyson allowed Gatty's interpretation to pass, though he corrected several of his other interpretations, goes for little, since he passed many more which are unquestionably wrong.[2]

On the other hand, if Tennyson were alluding to pre-existence here, we should certainly expect him to allude to it elsewhere in *In Memoriam*, and especially in the neighbouring sections. But we do not find these allusions, and we do find that in the very next section he assumes that the earthly life is the *first* individual life, and the earthly death the *second* birth, not the third or any larger number. Cf. too LXI. 1 and 10 : and also Epilogue, 123 f., where there is no hint of pre-existence. These facts form a very strong objection to view (*b*). Further (though I would not press this point if it stood alone), 'the hoarding sense' (6) presents a difficulty, as, on this view, it would imply that the soul has senses in the interval between two embodiments. Finally, the poet seems in this section to be appealing to

[1][Those who so interpret 'doorways' might appeal to a line in *The Princess*, VI. :

　　　　Or own one port of sense not flint to prayer.]

[2][Still, if he had *not* meant the sutures, surely Gatty's interpretation would have startled him, even supposing he had forgotten what he *had* meant.]

the analogy of some indubitable fact; and he never speaks of pre-existence as such a fact.

(*c*) The third view (if I understand it aright), like (*b*), takes stanza 2 to refer to pre-existence, but, like (*a*), understands by 'the days before,' etc., the infancy of the earthly life. This is the only interpretation I find in the commentators. Thus Gatty paraphrases: 'Here man continuously grows, but he forgets what happened . . . before the skull of the infant closed. Yet sometimes a little flash, a mystic hint, suggests the possibility of a previous existence.' And Genung: 'Our forgetfulness of infancy and pre-existence . . . . suggests a similar relation of the heavenly state to the earthly.'[1]

This interpretation seems to me almost impossible. It is open to the objections already urged against view (*b*), and in addition it makes 'the days' of line 3 and 'the days' of line 5 two distinct and separate periods, the first being the early months of earthly life, the second being a pre-earthly existence. This is surely a desperate expedient. I should say that two things at any rate are well-nigh certain about this passage : one, that 'the man' (2) and 'he' (3) are the same

[1] So apparently Beeching (in independence of his predecessors) : 'May not the dead forget the life here as we forget our babyhood? Even so, as we seem to have hints of a pre-natal life, some dim recollection of earth may penetrate into the life beyond.' I suppose Genung and Beeching understand the 'doorways' as Gatty does, but they do not say. [Mr. Beeching now thinks my interpretation correct.]

man; the other, that 'the days' (3) and 'the days'
(5) are the same days.

It is possible, however, to take a view resem-
bling this in some respects but free from its fatal
defect. We may boldly say that 'the days' of
line 3 are not distinct from, but a part of, and so
in a sense identical with, the 'days' of line 5.
Infancy, that is, is a part of pre-existence, not of
earthly existence.   Until the soul is self-conscious
on earth its earthly life in the proper sense has
not begun.   For in the next section we learn that
the baby is not at first a 'separate mind,' and
therefore has no 'clear memory': he only acquires
individuality and self-consciousness through isolation ; and his isolation grows defined by 'the
frame that binds him in.'   The closing of the
sutures then will be merely the most striking
example of this 'binding in.'   And the life of the
baby up to this point will belong to a pre-existent
life, and hence will be no more remembered than
that other part of the pre-existent life in which
the soul was not connected (as it is in a baby)
with an earthly body.

The relations, however, of these two parts of
pre-existence are troublesome. (1) Are we to
suppose that the soul, before it was a human
baby, lived a conscious life, in connection with a
body, which body then suffered death? This is
the obvious idea.   But if so, there is such a
marked separation between the two parts of the
pre-existence that 'the days' of lines 3 and 5

could hardly be spoken of as one period ; and so
the fatal defect of view (*c*) reappears.   (2) Or was
the soul, before it became a baby, what is called
in *The Two Voices* a 'naked essence,' which
'floated free' from any body ? If so, and if it had
any experience to remember (as *ex hyp.* it must
have, though scarcely an experience of 'sense'), it
was already a 'separate mind,' and could not need
a 'frame' to make it one.   (3) Or was the soul
in its previous state merged in, or undifferentiated
from, 'the general soul,' which particularises itself
into an individual soul by connection with a frame
or body (cf. XLVII. with XLV.) ?   It appears to me
quite likely that this is how Tennyson imagined
the matter ; but then this is not what is generally
meant by pre-existence, nor what Tennyson means
by it in *The Two Voices*, nor, I presume, what the
commentators mean; nor would there then be any
analogy, such as ought to be implied, between the
earthly man's forgetfulness of his previous existence, and the dead man's forgetfulness of his
earthly existence.

The reader will remember that, besides all this,
the objections already brought against view (*b*) are
equally valid against this modified form of view (*c*).
I have suggested this modified view mainly in order
to bring out the connection between the thought
of section XLV. and the meaning, as I understand
it, of XLIV. 3-6, for I do not believe that there is
any reference in the section to pre-existence.

I will end this discussion with a paraphrase

intended, unlike the opening paraphrase, to give the full meaning of the section. 'Perhaps at death the soul does not fall asleep, but begins at once a new conscious life. And perhaps in that life it has no remembrance of its earthly life. But as on earth the grown man, who has forgotten the experience of his infancy, may yet at times receive obscure intimations of it, so the soul in its next life, even if it has forgotten earthly things, may receive dim hints of them. If such a hint should reach my friend, let it be to him the germ from which a complete recollection may arise.'

1. 'happy' does not suggest that the dead are 'perchance too happy to think upon the things of Time.' It excludes the idea of sleep (XLIII.), and consideration of the unhappy dead.

2. 'more and more': cf. CXVIII. 17, and *Locksley Hall*, 'the world is more and more' (Robinson).

4. 'doorways.' Whether this refers to the organs of sense, or to the sutures, it remains a very strange expression. The image of the body as a house is familiar, and Tennyson often uses it (*e.g.*, in *The Deserted House, The Lover's Tale, Aylmer's Field*) ; nor is there anything very odd in the idea of the head as a house in which the soul sits. Then the eyes may be thought of as windows (as often in poetry), and the eyelids as eaves (LXVII. 11). And if Tennyson had been reading a book on the skull, in which he constantly met with words like 'arches,' 'walls,' 'roof,' he might easily go on to imagine the closing of the sutures as the shutting of folding-doors.[1] But a doorway is a passage by which entrances, or

[1] I add this sentence because of a suggestion made to me by Prof. L. C. Miall that Tennyson was influenced by the word 'arches,' familiar to anatomists in the forties in consequence of Owen's use of it. Prof. Miall hence understood 'the days,' etc., to mean 'the days before the arches of his skull were closed.'

exits, or both, are made. Perhaps then, if the doorways are the sutures, we are to imagine that at first the general soul goes freely in and out by these doorways, while later, when they are shut, some part of it, left inside, is the 'separate mind.' Section XLV., stanza 3, when compared with XLVII., stanza I (where notice '*re*merging'), would seem to point to some such image. Or again, the baby-soul may be pictured as at first going freely in and out. I cannot help suspecting that Tennyson was influenced by ideas about the world-soul, derived perhaps from Stoic or Neoplatonic writers (Hallam certainly read the latter). This discussion has run to such monstrous lengths that I will not pursue the suggestion, but I cherish the hope that the riddle of this phrase and of the whole section will some day be solved by the discovery of a Greek equivalent of 'doorways of his head.' The phrase has all the air of a reminiscence, but I have searched for its origin in vain.

[Prof. J. A. Stewart has called my attention to a significant story told in Plutarch's *De Genio Socratis*, 22, about a man who entered the cave of Trophonius. His soul left his body, saw many wonderful things, and returned to it again. It left and returned through the sutures, the opening and closing of which caused severe pain. It is just possible that the metaphor of 'door' was suggested by Aristotle's use of θύραθεν in a famous sentence, *de gen. an.*, 736 b 28.]

10. If at death a similar forgetfulness occurs. Cf. *Two Voices*:

> As old mythologies relate,
> Some draught of Lethe might await
> The slipping through from state to state.

12. 'ranging': cf. XCIII. 9.

14. The image is that of a man startled by some slight sound behind him or by a touch on the shoulder. If the friend turns, he will see the poet's guardian angel. With 'resolve the doubt,' cf. LXVIII. 12.

XLV.

An objection to the supposition of XLIV. 'After all we can hardly suppose that the soul in the next life has forgotten this life. For in that case it would not recognise *itself*, but would have to repeat the process of acquiring individuality and self-consciousness through which it went here. And in that case the purpose, or one purpose, of its embodiment here would be frustrated; for the use of the body was to form a self-conscious individual capable of clear memory. Hence the soul after death remembers itself, and therefore its past on earth. And so my friend can remember me.'

Probably it was the mention of infancy in XLIV. that set the poet thinking on the gradual formation of self-consciousness and memory. The difficulty of the section is due to his describing this process without indicating the bearing of the description until the last stanza.

In this poem, as in others down to the end of his life, Tennyson seems to imagine the soul as issuing from 'the general Soul' or 'the Infinite' or 'God,' as 'drawing from out the deep' (*Crossing the Bar, De Profundis*), or 'from out the vast' (*In Mem.*: Epilogue, 123), and 'striking its being into bounds' (*ib.*). The 'bounds' are due to the connection with 'matter,' 'the body,' 'blood and breath,' 'the frame'; and through it the soul gradually becomes 'a separate mind,' self-conscious, capable of memory, for memory deals 'but with time, And he with matter' (*Two Voices*). Cf. on CXX. 12.

8. 'And other': and am other.

9. 'rounds.' It seems impossible to make sure what metaphor is intended. The reverse process seems to be described in XLVII. 2, as 'moving his rounds,' for 'separate whole' must correspond to 'separate mind.' (1) 'Rounds he,' then, may mean 'becomes round, becomes an orb,' perhaps with the additional idea of detachment from the remaining nebular mass; in which case 'move his rounds' would mean 'allow his circular form to disappear,' as he lapses back into the nebula. Cf. 'orb' in XXIV. 15, and 'round' in *Eleanore*:

> As tho' a star, in inmost heaven set,
> Ev'n while we gaze on it,
> Should slowly round his orb, and slowly grow
> To a full face, there like a sun remain
> Fix'd—then as slowly fade again,
> And draw itself to what it was before;

and *The Princess*, II.,

> On the lecture slate
> The circle rounded under female hands.

(2) Or, both in the present passage and in XLVII., 'rounds' may refer merely to movement in an orbit: 'moving round he gradually becomes a separate whole,' and 'should, as he moves round, fuse all the skirts,' etc. Cf. LXIII. 11. 'Round' is also used of movement, not change of shape, in *Mariana in the South*:

> And slowly rounded to the east
> The one black shadow from the wall.

Cf. 'orbit of the memory,' in *The Gardener's Daughter*, and 'we . . . rounded by the stillness of the beach,' in *Audley Court*. And Milton often uses the substantive and the verb thus: e.g. *Par. Lost*, IV. 685, 862; VIII. 125. But (3) the word *need* not have the same meaning in the two passages. 'Rounds he' may='becomes round,' and 'move his rounds' may='move round.' And I suspect this is the right interpretation, though, if so, it is strange that Tennyson, in writing the second passage, should not have noticed the difficulty he was causing.

11. Cf. XLIV. 4. 'frame': used as in Epilogue, 11.

13. Cf. *King John*, IV. ii. 246, 'This kingdom, this confine of blood and breath.'

14. There seems to be a mixture of two constructions: 'This use may lie in blood and breath, which otherwise (but for this use) would not bear their due fruit,' and 'This use may lie in blood and breath, which would not bear their due fruit (would be useless) if man had to learn himself anew.'

XLVI.

'Here on earth our memory is imperfect, because the interest of the present and future overshadows the past. And this must be so, because otherwise our life would be absorbed in the past, and we should not advance. But in the next life this reason for the imperfectness of memory will not exist. The past from birth to death will be seen clearly, and the five years of friendship will be seen as its richest field. Nay, let the whole of life, not only those five years, appear as the realm of Love.'

I have paraphrased the section, but I am uncertain of the meaning of the last two stanzas. The sections of this group are otherwise so closely connected that we expect to find here something bearing on the question of memory in the next life, considered as a necessary condition of the poet's reunion with his friend. And in the first two stanzas we seem to find this. The poet in XLV. has persuaded himself that the dead remember. Now the thought seems to occur to him that here on earth, though we remember the past, our memory is very imperfect, and that accordingly the memory of the dead also may be imperfect ; from which it would follow that his friend after all may not remember him. To this he answers that there is a good reason why memory on earth should be dim and broken, and that this reason does not hold of the next life. But the 'shall' in line 7, and still more the next two stanzas, show that he is not thinking of his friend's present state, but of some future time when in another life someone will look back on the earthly life and the five years of friendship. And it is not clear who this someone is—himself, or his friend, or both of them ; and still less clear is the meaning of the last stanza, which appears to correct something said in stanza 3 (see the paraphrase above).

Of the commentators, Genung says : 'The lifetime which Arthur remembers may perhaps show those five years of friendship as its richest period, lending radiance to all the rest.' But this interpretation seems impossible, not only for the reason given above, but also (1) because, according to it, Arthur is asked, in stanza 4, to regard in the light of Love, not only the five years of friendship

which terminated his short life, but the preceding
years in which he did not know the poet at all ;
and (2) because on this view stanza 3 is the
description of a life ended in youth, and it certainly does not read like this.   Miss Chapman
thinks that the poet is speaking of himself
throughout.   Her paraphrase runs thus : ' He
prays that his love for his lost friend may dwell
with him to the very end of life—not sorrowfully,
or his life's work could not be done—but still ever
in his heart.   So that, looking back upon this life
from out the clearness and the calm of the other,
it may appear all tinged with roseate hues of love
—all—not the five rich years of friendship only.'
Here the first stanza is certainly misinterpreted,
and so the connection with the group is lost ; but
otherwise the paraphrase appears to give the least
improbable sense.   I suppose Tennyson inserted
the section here because the opening argument
about memory deals with the question whether
the dead can remember their earthly life, and
in spite of the fact that the argument is then
applied to his own case, not Hallam's, and ends
in an exhortation to himself regarding his present
life.

A less probable idea is that in the last three
stanzas the poet is thinking of the time when he
will rejoin his friend, and they will together look
back on the past.   This would explain the future
' shall,' and would provide a connection with XLVII.
(see especially lines 8-10), the thought of re-

union in XLVI. suggesting the idea, 'But perhaps after all the soul loses its individuality at death.' Stanza 4 might then be taken somewhat as Miss Chapman takes it: 'let me see that, when we look back on our lives, the *whole* of my life shall show itself irradiated by Love'; or possibly 'Love' might be the loving memory of the two friends, looking back not only to the five years, but to the whole of the poet's life. (Either interpretation would suggest that the dead friend is *now* aware of his friend's life on earth : cf. last stanza of XLIV.).

[Robinson takes the person contemplating to be the departed friend, but the life contemplated to be the poet's. The last stanza would then mean : 'when he comes to look back on my completed life, may the whole of it appear irradiated by my love for him'; and this wish might suggest the thought, 'But, when that time comes, we shall look back together,' and so lead to XLVII. I had considered this interpretation, but had rejected it as too improbable.

It has been suggested to me that the main contrast in the last stanza is not really between the five years and the whole life, but between memory and present love. In the next life there will be not only the *recollection* of the love that enriched a part of the past, but also a present *feeling* of love which will colour the view of the whole past. The first three stanzas say, 'we shall remember'; the last adds, 'we shall love one another too.' If this interpretation is correct, I should suppose the poet was thinking both of himself and of his friend. It connects the section well with its successor, and it also leads back to the idea of XLII., last stanza, and XLIII., last stanza —an idea from which the poet was diverted by his question, ' But do the dead remember the earthly life ? ']

2. See Introduction, p. 7.

3. Cf. one of Tennyson's earliest poems, *Memory*, in *Poems by Two Brothers* :

> Days of youth, now shaded
> By twilight of long years.

'growing hour' : occurs also in *Love thou thy land*.

5 foll. Here, and in the next section, the second life seems to be thought of as simply a time of rest and fruition. This is not usual with Tennyson, but is necessary to the argument of this unfortunate section.

7. 'from marge to marge' : from birth to death. Cf. 16.

13, 14. The 'bounded field' must be the 'field' of 12. It has been suggested that ' O Love' is an address to the dead friend ; but this does not seem to be in keeping with the tone of *In Memoriam*, even in its most emotional passages, such as CXXIX.

XLVII.

This section, which closes the group, rejects the 'vast' but 'vague' idea that after death the soul is remerged in 'the general Soul.' The soul will always retain its individuality, and the friends will know one another and be together for ever. Or if not this, yet the least that Love, as we know it on earth, demands is that, before we 'lose ourselves in light,' we should meet again to say farewell.

Here the appeal is to the demand of Love (cf. XLVI. 13-16). A different ground of objection is taken in the words recorded in the *Memoir*, I. 319: 'If the absorption into the divine in the after-life be the creed of some, let them at all events allow us many existences of individuality before this absorption, since this short-lived individuality seems to be but too short a preparation for so mighty a union.' With the last words cf. 'vaster dream' (11). See p. 53.

The lines in the *Dedicatory Poem to the Princess Alice*,

> if what we call
> The spirit flash not all at once from out
> This shadow into Substance,

seem at first to refer to this 'absorption into the divine,' but I think the idea is rather that, for a time after death, the soul may retain traces of its earthly existence, where it was surrounded by shadows or appearances, but that later it loses these traces and becomes wholly real or substantial, without, however, losing its individuality. This notion of a gradual separation from earthly life appears elsewhere in Tennyson, *e.g.* in *The Ring*.

2-4. See on XLV. 9. 'Again' and 'remerging' imply the emergence from the general Soul described in XLV.

13. The 'last and sharpest height' corresponds to the last of the 'many existences of individuality.' Cf. 'From state to state the spirit walks' (LXXXII. 6), and XXX. 27, 28. The

metaphor here is that of the topmost peak of a mountain surrounded with sunlight. 'Landing-place' seems not to suit it.

SECTIONS XLVIII.-XLIX.

He breaks off and warns the reader neither to take his songs for a serious discussion of problems, nor to blame them for their fancifulness. His deeper thought and deepest sorrow are silent. There is a special reference to the group just concluded, and the 'doubts,' 'hopes,' and 'fears' expressed in it.

For the contrast of the deeper silent grief and the 'lighter moods,' cf. XIX., XX.: for earlier sections dealing with his poems, cf. V., VIII., XXI., XXXVII., XXXVIII.

XLVIII.

2. 'closed': 'concluded, disposed of,' or perhaps 'enclosed, contained,' as in *The Princess*, Conclusion,

> few words and pithy, such as closed
> Welcome, farewell, and welcome for the year
> To follow.

In either case the poet implies that the doubts and answers of the foregoing sections make no claim to be proposed and discussed with the seriousness of philosophy. Cf. 7, and XLIX. 13.

5. 'part': analyse.

7-9. Cf. CXXV.

8. As in XLII., XLIII., XLVI., XLVII. (Eve). Cf. Shakespeare, Sonnet 26, 'Lord of my love, to whom in vassalage' (Beeching).

K

10. The meaning seems to be, not: 'does better still when, following a wholesome law, she holds it,' etc., but : 'is more true to a wholesome law when she refrains from drawing the deepest measure from the chords than she would be if she did draw it.'   Mr. Ferrall suggests another interpretation : 'True, Sorrow merely sports with words, but in doing so she at the same time serves a better purpose and observes a wholesome law ; and if she trifles, it is because she holds it,' etc., the use of 'better' being somewhat like Milton's in 'last in the train of night, If better thou belong not to the dawn,' *Par. Lost*, V. 167.

16. 'tears': this suggests the metaphor of the next section, with which cf. XVI. 5 ff.

XLIX.

1. 'the schools' : of theology and philosophy.

5. 'lightest' : the poet did not notice that he had used 'light' in 3.

8. 'crisp': 'curl,' 'ripple,' a verb.   Cf. *Par. Lost*, IV. 237, 'the crisped brooks.'   The word occurs often in Tennyson's early poems, *e.g.* 'To watch the crisping ripples on the beach' (*Lotos-Eaters*).

9. He addresses the traveller, as in XXI.

16. 'bases' : the metaphor seems to be changed.

SECTIONS L.-LVI.

These seven poems are united into a group by certain characteristics. (1) They start from, and return to (LVI. 26), the poet's desire for *present* communion with his friend, a desire which has scarcely appeared up to this point. (2) The main subject, however, is not this present communion but the pain, defect, and evil in the world, and the doubts which they cast upon the faith that Love is ' Creation's final law ' and that man is not made to die. The problem is first suggested by the poet's consciousness of his own defect, is then rapidly generalised (LIV.), and finally concentrates itself again on the question of immortality (LV., LVI.). (3) Naturally, some of these poems are more passionate and ' wild ' (LVII., 4) than those of the preceding group, so that the apology of XLVIII., XLIX., would be inappropriate in reference to them.

L.

Some of the opening sections of *Maud* express dramatically, but with much less concentration, the mood described in this famous section. Cf. also with stanza 1 the lines in *The Two Voices* :

> 'Tis life, whereof our nerves are scant,
> Oh life, not death, for which we pant ;
> More life, and fuller, that I want.

10. **The summer-fly of Shakespeare and Milton** (*Samson*, 676).

11. ' **sting and sing.**' The contemptuous rhyme is perhaps an unconscious reminiscence of Pope's couplet (*Epistle to Dr. Arbuthnot*, 309) :

> Yet let me flap this bug with gilded wings,
> This painted child of dirt, that stinks and stings.

14. ' point the term ' : point to the limit.

15, 16. Cf. xcv. 63, 64.

LI.

' Though he shares that baseness of men which sometimes almost destroys his faith (L., st. 3), he still wishes his friend to be near him always. The dead, who see all, can make allowance for all.' On the date of composition, see p. 16.

10. 'Shall I who love him be guilty of a want of faith that would incur his blame?' not, I think, 'He will not blame a want of faith which arises from love'; nor, 'Shall I ascribe to one who loves me a blameable want of faith?' nor, 'Shall I, owing to my want of faith, find something blameworthy in one who loves me?' The obscurity is due partly to the fact that ' love' recalls ' love' in 8, while ' blamed' recalls ' blame' in 6.

LII.

' His own imperfection, even the imperfection of his love, must not weaken his faith. No ideal can keep its worshipper wholly true to it, yet his worship remains in spite of defects. These will drop away one day : good is the final goal of ill.'

1-5. The first lines seem at first to refer merely to his poems. ' It cannot be that I truly love thee, for if I did, my words would give a true image of thee instead of being mere words,' those records of superficial moods which he has so often declared them to be (the metaphor in 2 may be due to the image in XLIX.). But probably the meaning of lines 1 and 2 is more general : ' If I truly loved thee I should be more like thee, not so full of imperfection' (see LI.) ; and this suggests his poems, the most obvious instance of his failing to ' reflect the thing beloved.'

4. Collins quotes Persius, *Sat.* I. 104, ' Summa delumbe saliva Hoc natat in labris'; cf. note on XVIII. 3, 4.

11. 'not,' etc. : not even the record of the highest ideal.

16. 'shell' and 'pearl': not 'flesh' and 'soul' (Gatty), but the worthless and the precious in him.

LIII.

'Perhaps evil is even sometimes the way to good, though this doctrine may easily lead to evil rather than good.' For the sake of the connection I have emphasised the 'doctrine,' but what the poem emphasises is the danger of it. Perhaps the section was suggested by the metaphor of the last line of LII., and the reflection, 'No shell, no pearl.' Cf. *Love and Duty* :

> Shall Error in the round of Time
> Still father Truth? O shall the braggart shout
> For some blind glimpse of freedom work itself
> Thro' madness, hated by the wise, to law
> System and empire? Sin itself be found
> The cloudy porch oft opening on the Sun?

and *Measure for Measure*, v. i. 444 f. (quoted by Robinson) :

> They say, best men are moulded out of faults,
> And, for the most, become much more the better
> For being a little bad.

5. 'fancy': first ed. : 'doctrine.'

'give': yield. Tennyson is fond of this use of 'give.'

7. 'scarce had': first ed.: 'had not.' The alteration shows the poet's shrinking from the 'doctrine.' For the metaphor cf. *2 Henry IV.*, IV. iv. 54 (of Prince Henry),

> Most subject is the fattest soil to weeds.

9-12. The fear of doing harm by the public mention of subjects and ideas which (he considered) could only be safely discussed by the few, was evidently a marked characteristic of Tennyson.

9. 'Or, if': first ed. : 'Oh, if' (a late change).

13. 'Even if evil is sometimes the condition of good, that does not lessen the difference between them. Hold to the good, and make its nature clear to yourself.' This warning has not saved the author from being represented as trusting that 'error and folly and sin and suffering are "good, only misunderstood."'

14. Cf. *Comus*, 476, 'divine philosophy,' and XXIII. 22.

LIV.

'We trust that good will be the final goal of *all* evil, and that in the end no life will prove to be wasted or destroyed. But we know nothing, we have but blind trust, or even less—blind longing.'

He has been led on from his own defects to consider evil in all its forms.

1. 'Oh yet': though we hesitate to accept the 'doctrine' of LIII. (Ferrall).

3, 4. 'pangs of nature,' cf. L. 5, 6 ; 'sins of will,' cf. LI. 3, 4, LIII. 6, 16 ; 'defects of doubt,' cf. L. and LI. 9, 10 : 'taints of blood,' cf. III. 15 with L. 7-12.

7. Like the 'shell' of LII. 16.   He is returning to the problem of life beyond the grave (see LV.).

9-12. This stanza, in its connection with those that precede and follow it, implies a trust that in the end 'good shall fall to animals as well as men ; but I know no sign elsewhere in Tennyson's poems of an idea that animals may live again, or in some other way find their pain and death 'gain' to them. Cf. note on LV. 20.

12. 'but': merely.

13. Cf. Prologue, 21.

15. 'at last': at the 'far-off divine event' of the last lines of *In Memoriam.* Cf. *Two Voices* :

> He seems to hear a Heavenly Friend,
> And thro' thick veils to apprehend
> A labour working to an end.

18. Cf. CXXIV. 19.

20. Not able even to say what it is he cries for. For the simile cf. Herbert, *The Collar.*

LV.

'This desire that no life should fail beyond the grave seems to be a divine instinct in us, for Nature appears so careless of individual life that she lends it no support; nay, her testimony seems so hostile that he can barely sustain a dumb trust in the divine Love which he feels to be Lord of all.'

On the ideas of this section and the next see Introduction, pp. 55 ff., and *Memoir*, I. 312 ff.

7, 8. 'La nature s'embarrasse peu des individus, elle ne s'occupe que de l'espèce' : Buffon.

14, 15. Cf. Sophocles, *Antig.* 853.

16. 'darkness' : cf. CXXIV. 23. Cf. and contrast *Princess,* VII. :

> For she that out of Lethe scales with man
> The shining steps of Nature.

18. 'And gather dust and chaff' : in trying to reason. Cf. *Two Voices* : 'a dust of systems and of creeds.'

19. Cf. Prologue, stanza 2.

20. 'the larger hope' : 'he means by "the larger hope" that the whole human race would through, perhaps, ages of suffering, be at length purified and saved,' *Memoir,* I. 321. Is this also the 'divine event'?

LVI.

'Nature seems to care for the kind no more than the individual, to produce life and death with equal indifference, to set no value on the spiritual achievement and possibilities of man, and therefore to promise him only extinction. If so, his life is a hideous and futile self-contradiction. But there is no solution of this riddle for us on earth.'

With the passionate distress of this section should be contrasted the tone of XXXIV., where the same subject was approached, but the confidence in immortality was undisturbed.

1. See LV. 7.

2. Cliff and quarry are full of the fossils of extinct species.

'scarped': cut away vertically so as to expose the strata.

7. 'spirit,' and all that it does and promises (10-18).

9 ff. For the poet's own belief see CXVIII.

11. 'wintry' answers to 'fruitless' in 12. Cf. LIV. 16. The idea, as the next stanza shows, is that the apparent fruitlessness of his praises and prayers did not shake his faith.

20. Like any other fossil.

21. 'No more?' refers back to line 8, the idea of which must be taken to include the consequences drawn from it in stanzas 3-5.

'A monster,' etc. If all that we count highest in man ends in extinction, his nature is that of the monsters of fiction, or such an incongruous combination as occurs in a dream. The 'dragon' of the first ages of the earth may seem horrible to us, but at least it was in harmony with itself. The point is not that man, if doomed to extinction, would be in discord with the rest of Nature, but that he would be in discord with himself. The conclusion here, also, is not that such a self-contradictory being is impossible, but that man's life, if he were such, would be as futile as we know it to be frail. With the dragon cf. the 'monstrous eft' of *Maud*, I. iv.; with 'prime,' *The Princess*, II., of primitive man, 'Raw from the prime.'

27. 'answer': cf. the conclusion of the *Vision of Sin* (Eve). 'Redress': for the injustice of this futile existence. Cf. Prologue 12.

28. The general meaning of this line is not doubtful, but it is impossible to say what metaphor was in the poet's mind. He may have thought of 'the holy place within the veil, before the mercy-seat which is upon the ark,' *Levit.* xvi. 2, with which cf. *Heb.* vi. 19, 20. But it seems more probable that he refers to the inscription at Sais containing the words, 'No one has lifted my veil': for cf. in the section of *Maud* just quoted,

For the drift of the Maker is dark, an Isis hid by the veil;

and for the image of a veiled statue cf. ciii. 12. In *De Profundis* the words,

our mortal veil

And shatter'd phantom of that Infinite One,

seem to describe the world of space and time. See also note on LIV. 15 for a quotation from *The Two Voices*. In any case the idea is that the 'veil' can never be removed in this life.

LVII.

As so often at the close of a group, the poet pauses to consider what he has just said. The wildness of his songs, he feels, is a wrong to the grave. They will not perpetuate the memory of his friend, since they will soon be forgotten; and they only sadden those who hear them. He calls these fellow-mourners to come away from the grave over which they have been singing. He will come too, but to the end of life he will always be silently repeating his farewell.

On the position of this section in the elegy see Introduction, pp. 28, 29.

In the *Memoir*, I. 306, there is printed a section called ' *The Grave* (originally No. LVII.),' which begins :

> I keep no more a lone distress,
>> The crowd have come to see thy grave,
>> Small thanks or credit shall I have,
> But these shall see it none the less.

This stanza helps to explain the second stanza of the present poem, which was, I presume, substituted for *The Grave*.

The contrast between the style of the first two stanzas and that of the last two is very effective. The former has no exact parallel in *In Memoriam*, but there is an approach to it in LXIX., parts of XCVII., XXX., stanzas 3, 4, 5, which contrast with 6, 7.

2. Cf. XXXVII. 13 (Robinson).

4. 'wildly': cf. Prologue, 41.

7, 8. 'richly shrined': in these poems. ' Methinks I have built a rich shrine for my friend, but it will not last' (authoritative correction in Gatty, p. 62). Cf. LXXV., LXXVI., LXXVII. 'fail': die away, as in II. 15, XXVIII. 7, XLVI. 4, LXXXIV. 36.

9f. G. A. C. compares *2 Henry IV.*, I. i. 102 :

> Sounds ever after as a sullen bell
> Remember'd tolling a departing friend.

14. 'greetings' : 'Ave' in the next line means 'greeting' or 'hail.'

15, 16. Catullus, at his brother's grave, 'Atque in perpetuum, frater, ave atque vale' (C. 10); of which line Tennyson writes ; 'nor can any modern elegy, so long as men retain the least hope in the after-life of those whom they loved, equal in pathos the desolation of that everlasting farewell' (*Memoir*, II. 239). With the thrice-repeated *Ave* cf. *Aen.* VI. 506, 'et magna manes ter voce vocavi.' 'For evermore' in 16 does not go with 'Adieu,' as Gatty supposes, but with 'said.' The inverted commas, and the context from 9 onward, make this certain. Contrast with these lines CXXIII. 11, 12.

LVIII.

'No, he will not leave the grave with this hopeless farewell, which only brings grief to others. Some day he will take a nobler leave.'

The distress of the sections preceding LVII. was continued in the deep sadness of that section. On the change in the tone of the poem from this point, see pp. 28, 29.

1. 'those sad words' : the 'greetings' of the end of LVII.

3. Cf. *The Lover's Tale* :

> While her words, syllable by syllable,
> Like water, drop by drop, upon my ear
> Fell.

6, 7. The fellow-mourners or by-standers of LVII.   'Half-conscious' : only half-conscious.

9. Possibly, as Robinson suggests, he thinks here of Urania (XXXVII. 1), as of Melpomene in LVII. 2.

11. 'here' : by the grave.

LIX.

This section was added in the fourth edition, 1851. Cf. with it LXVI. and contrast III.

He attempts again to 'embrace' Sorrow 'as his natural good' (Robinson).

Cf. *Richard II.*, v. i. 93, and *King John*, III. iv. 34 (G. A. C.); also Shelley's *Misery*, beginning:

> Come, be happy, sit near me,
> Shadow-vested Misery,
> Coy, unwilling, silent bride;

and the Song to Sorrow in *Endymion*, IV.

1, 5. 'Wilt thou': if thou wilt.

6, 7. 'be,' 'put,' are imperatives. 'Harsher moods': repeated, probably unconsciously, from XLVIII. 6.

13. 'set thee forth': deck thee out (unless the metaphor is dropped).

SECTIONS LX.-LXV.

This group of quiet and beautiful poems recalls in some ways the earlier group XL.-XLVII.; but there the motive idea was that of future reunion, while here the poems deal with the present relation of the friends and the poet's desire that his friend should think of him now. This desire is alternately repressed and encouraged in the first five sections; it comes to rest for a time in LXV. The mere connection of the poems may be shown in the following summary. 'How can he think of one so far below him (LX.)? Yet let him think of me; for, inferior as I am, not the greatest of the dead can love him more (LXI.). Still, if thinking of me holds him back, let him forget me (LXII.). But why should it hold him back (LXIII.)? Perhaps he may remember me at long intervals and dimly—perhaps not at all (LXIV.). Whether he remembers me or not, our love on earth may still help him as it helps me (LXV.).' The growth of resignation in the series is seen also in the difference between the kinds of affection spoken of in the similes of the earlier and the later sections.

The poems of this group are criticised by some readers on the ground that they are written in a tone of excessive and unnatural humility. The criticism is perhaps not totally unjustified, but such readers seem to forget that the poet's friend is almost throughout imagined as he is in that 'second state sublime' which the poet conceives to be far superior to the earthly state in which he himself remains. Tennyson himself had to point this out in connection with XCVII.

LX.

1. 'nobler': not 'nobler than mine,' but 'very noble' (Beeching). This use of the comparative is a Latinism which was introduced by Spenser and other Elizabethans but has never become English.

LXI.

1. 'state sublime': Robinson quotes Gray's *Ode for Music*, II., a passage which evidently influenced Tennyson here.

2. 'ransom'd': cf. XXXVIII. 10, 'spirits render'd free.'

6. The metaphor of the flower (4) is continued. 'Character'd': marked: see on XLIII. 11. The word is not uncommon in Shakespeare; *e.g.*, *As You Like It*, III. ii. 6:

> these trees shall be my books,
> And in their barks my thoughts I'll character.

9. 'doubtful': see XLIV. 14. Here there is the additional idea of darkness, coming from the preceding stanza.

10. See I. 'Where thou wast first embodied, and that in human form.' Cf. pp. 51, 131.

12. 'Shakespeare': the greatest of intellects and the devoted lover of a friend.

LXII.

1. See LXI. 5. 'Tho'' in effect = 'yet,' which was used four lines above.

2. 'blench': flinch; 'fail': the idea is that of losing the power to advance, as in XLVI. 4.

3. 'Then': first ed.: 'So.'

4. Cf. *Faust, Zueignung*:

> Gleich einer alten, halbverklungnen Sage,
> Kommt erste Lieb' und Freundschaft mit herauf.

5. 'declined': cf. *Hamlet*, I. v. 50:

> To decline
> Upon a wretch whose natural gifts were poor
> To those of mine,

and *Locksley Hall*,

> having known me, to decline
> On a range of lower feelings and a narrower heart than mine.

LXIII.

10 ff. The metaphor is that of a planet with a larger orbit than the earth's. It may, but does not necessarily, imply that the soul of the dead is re-embodied on such a planet or 'orb' (XXX. 28). For 'round,' see on XLV. 9

LXIV.

Said by an old friend of Tennyson's to have been composed while the author was walking down the Strand. *In Memoriam* contains greater poems, but none perhaps more exquisitely imagined and written. For the structure, see note on XIV.

10. 'golden keys' of State office. Cf. Shelley, *Hellas*, 'Or bears the sword, or grasps the key of gold.' Perhaps Tennyson had just read Macaulay's vivid description of the Duke of Devonshire (Lord Chamberlain) tearing off his gold key on receiving an insulting message from the King. (*The Earl of Chatham, Edinburgh Review*, Oct., 1844.)

25 f. The pathetic effect is increased by the fact that in the two preceding stanzas we are not told that his old friend does remember him.

LXV.

Perhaps the first section of *In Memoriam* that can be described as cheerful or happy. The beauty of this happiness is the more felt because the reader expects the poet's doubts of being remembered to end in sadness. The 'point' of the section is frequently missed. It is nowhere said or implied that 'the two friends, though separated, partake of the same hallowed remembrance.' On the contrary the poet, dismissing his troubled doubts about *remembrance*, finds comfort in the thoughts, 'Love cannot be lost,' and 'Since the *effect* of our friendship works so strongly in me, it may work also in him.'

1. 'Sweet soul': cf. LVII. 11. 'Do with me': remember me or forget me.

4. Not even a little grain shall be spilt. For 'grain,' used of his love for his friend, cf. LXXXI.

5-7. 'painful phases': the painful doubt of being remembered. 'Metaphor from butterfly and chrysalis' (Beeching).

11. 'a part of mine': the idea seems to be, 'Since your influence on me remains so strong, perhaps *some* influence of mine on you may remain.'

LXVI.

Addressed to a friend who wonders at the change in him. He is like a blind man, who is kindly and pleased with trifles, though he dwells in a world of his own where the night of vision and the day of thought never change.

The section is happily placed. By recalling LIX. it marks the close of the group which began with LX.; while the picture of the blind man prepares for the inner world of dreams which is about to open.

SECTIONS LXVII.-LXXI.

These five sections do not deal with one subject or phase of feeling, but they are doubtless placed together because they refer to night, sleep, or dreams. They are all descriptive rather than reflective, LXVII. and LXX. being, in their very different ways, among the finest of the descriptive sections of *In Memoriam*. All or nearly all show the softening of sorrow, and the growing sense of the beauty of the past.　Contrast IV. and XIII.

LXVII.

See Introduction, p. 3, and sections XVIII., XIX.

In *Poems by Two Brothers* there are some verses, doubtfully ascribed to A. T., *On the Moonlight shining upon a Friend's Grave*; and passages in *The Walk at Midnight* and *On Sublimity* are also worth comparing with this section.

5. 'bright in dark': cf. Shakespeare, Son. 43, 'And darkly bright are bright in dark directed' (Collins).　The moonlight is imagined coming through a narrow window.

11. 'eaves': the metaphor recurs in *Clear-headed friend* and *Tiresias* ('the roofs of sight'), the word in 'Her eyelids dropp'd their silken eaves,' *The Talking Oak.*

15. 'dark church': first ed.: 'chancel.'　'I myself did not see Clevedon till years after the burial of A. H. H., Jan. 3rd, 1834, and then in later editions of "In Memoriam" I altered the word "chancel," which was the word used by Mr. Hallam in his Memoir, to "dark church."' (Tennyson in *Memoir*, I. 305).　The tablet is 'in the manor aisle' (*ib.* 295).　The inscription is given in the *Memoir* (*ib.* 296) and also in Gatty.　The alteration improves the poem, as 'dark church' recalls the picture of line 5.

LXVIII.

2. Homer calls sleep the brother of death, *Il.* XIV. 231.

5. Cf. 'In sleep she seem'd to walk forlorn,' *Mariana.*

6. 'path': cf. XXII. ff.

9. 'turn about': cf. XLIV. 14, where also 'resolve the doubt' (12 of this section) occurs.　For the sense of confusion cf. IV.

13. For the early waking of grief cf. VII.

15, 16. 'my youth': see Introduction, p. 16. For the idea of the dreamer's feeling 'ideally transferred' to the person dreamed of, cf. *The Lover's Tale*, II., end of paragraph beginning 'Alway.'

LXIX.

It is not likely that the reader is expected to interpret the details of the dream ; but the main idea evidently is that the poet's acceptance of sorrow, which seems folly to the world, is approved by higher knowledge. If nowhere else, yet in the crown of thorns itself, the winter which he thought eternal changes to spring (LIV. 16), and though he can hardly understand the words he hears (for they are in the language of another world), the voice is 'not the voice of grief.'

For the crown, cf. the metaphor in CXVIII. 18, 'crown'd with attributes of woe Like glories. It does not seem likely that the crown of thorns is 'the heritage of prophet and martyr,' or that it is transformed into 'a victor's crown' (Chapman). There is a reference to his poems on his sorrow : cf. XXI.

For the short sentences cf. note on LVII.

8. 'civic crown': a sign of honour.

14. Not simply 'I found an angel as I wandered in the night,' nor 'such an angel as comes to us in dreams,' but 'one of the angels of the night of sorrow,' 'the divine Thing in the gloom' (Tennyson's words to Mr. Knowles).

19, 20. Cf. for the message of comfort, 'hard to understand,' the second voice, with its 'notice faintly understood,' of *The Two Voices*, and the mysterious close of the *Vision of Sin*.

LXX.

1 f. Cf. Browne, *Rel. Med.* II. 6 : 'Whom we truly love like our own selves, we forget their looks, nor can our memory retain the idea of their faces' (G. A. C.).

2. See Introduction, p. 7.

4. 'hollow': empty, void of substance: cf. III. 11, 12. 'Masks': false appearances, as in XVIII. 10. Cf. 'Her college and her maidens, empty masks,' *Princess*, III.

8. Cf. πολλὰς δ' ὁδοὺς ἐλθόντα φροντίδος πλάνοις, Soph. *O.T.* 67 (see Mrs. Shelley's note to *Prometheus Unbound*).

13. 'beyond the will': see 2. As the striving ceases and sleep comes on, there appear first the 'masks'; then, when sleep is complete, the image he could not picture. Cf. IV. 2.

LXXI.

2. 'madness : suggested by the 'masks' of LXX.

4. See the lines *In the Valley of Cauteretz*. The year was 1830. 'In the summer my father joined Arthur Hallam, and both started off for the Pyrenees, with money for the insurgent allies of Torrijos. . . . He it was who had raised the standard of revolt against the Inquisition and the tyranny of Ferdinand, King of Spain' (*Memoir*, I. 51). Cf. l. 11.

5. 'such credit': such acceptance as to produce an illusion so strong.

6. First ed. : 'So bring an opiate treble-strong.'

7. Even this dream had been troubled like that of LXVIII. For 'sense of wrong' cf. the last three stanzas of the next section, and LXXXII. 14.

8. First ed.: 'That thus my pleasure might be whole.'

15. I suppose, as they look up the torrent towards the bridge, the fall under the bridge appears to flash from the darker arch itself. Some construe: 'the cataract flashing as we watch it from the bridge.' But cf. *Aylmer's Field* (of the *noyades*): 'naked marriages Flash from the bridge.'

LXXII.

The first anniversary of his friend's death (Sept. 15). Contrast XCIX. The effect of this splendid, if somewhat rhetorical, outburst of wrath, in which the day is pursued with invective through its monstrous life of criminal violence to its dull and shameful close, is enhanced by contrast with the calm of the fourteen preceding sections. The third stanza seems hardly in keeping with the tone of the poem.

3. 'white': by turning up the under-side of the leaves. So of the willow and the olive in *The Lady of Shalott* (st. 2) and *The Palace of Art* (st. 20). Cf. *Hamlet*, IV. vii. 168.

5. 'Day': the word is repeated throughout the poem almost as if it were a term of reproach.

'crown'd': cf. XXII. 6.

16. 'Along the hills': first ed.: 'From hill to hill.'

'yet look'd': and yet would'st have looked.

19, 20. For the moment he figures the world as ruled by a blind or malicious Fate. Cf. perhaps 6. Contrast LXXXV. 20, CXXIV. 23, 24.

27. 'Alludes to the hour of noon when the sun reaches its highest point' (C. E. Benham). With Gatty, I should take the line with 28 as referring to sunset.

28. Cf. Shakespeare, Sonnet 33, 'Stealing unseen to west with this disgrace.'

SECTIONS LXXIII.-LXXVII.

The subject of this group is Fame. The passion of LXXII. dies away, but perhaps it is the lingering sense of wrong that turns the poet's thoughts to the fame lost to his friend by an early death. From this he passes to the shortness of any fame which he could give to his friend by his verses.

Cf. *Lycidas*, 70 ff.

LXXIII.

He does not complain because the earth has lost what his friend would have given it : some other world has gained by the loss. Nor does he accuse nature because his friend has missed the fame the earth would have given him : nature obeys her law. Nor will he regret this loss of earthly fame : it is a thing that dies, while the soul of the dead retains the force that would have earned it.

1-4. Cf. XXX. 25-28, XL. 17-20, LXXXII. 9-12.

7. Perhaps a reference to LXXII.

12. Cf. *Lycidas*, 81 ff.

13, 14. 'hollow' : see LXX. 4. In Tennyson's mind the ideas of immortality and of the highest worth seem to be inseparable. If love is the best of things it cannot die, and, conversely, that which dies or is lost through death cannot be of the highest value. Just as human life seems to him not worth having if the soul that lives it is not immortal, so the vanity of earthly fame seems to him to follow at once from its brevity.

15, 16. Cf. *Ode on the Death of the Duke of Wellington*:

> Gone ; but nothing can bereave him
> Of the force he made his own
> Being here.

[Mr. Eve thinks there is an allusion to the idea of potential energy. If this were so, it would give a late date to the section.]

LXXIV.

He realises more and more the 'strength' and 'force' (LXXIII. 4, 16) which would have won for his friend a fame on earth like that of its great men of old. But he will not speak of that which was never fully shown here, and now brightens another world.

This seems to be the idea expressed in the last stanza, and serving to connect the section with LXXIII. and LXXV. (see LXXV. 13-20).

1-4. Gatty quotes Browne, *Letter to a Friend*, of some one recently dead [it is really of some one near death]: 'he lost his own face . . . and looked like his uncle.'

7, 8. Cf. LXI. 'Below' surely means 'among the dead,' not 'now on earth.'

9. Refers to 6. Even yet he cannot realise *all* the likeness and greatness.

11, 12. Cf. the famous soliloquy in *Romeo and Juliet*, v. iii. 74 ff. Collins compares Petrarch, Sonnet 80,

> Non può far Morte il dolce viso amaro,
> Ma 'l dolce viso dolce può far Morte.

LXXV.

2. 'in a poem which is written only to relieve my sorrow,' rather than 'though to sing thy praise would bring me relief.' Cf. LXXVII. stanza 4.

9. 'these fading days': this transitory element of time: he does not refer to his own time in particular. 'Fading' may be suggested by the 'dying' and 'fading' of LXXIII. 13, 14.

11. 'breeze of song': cf. οὖρος ὕμνων, Pindar, *Pyth.* 4, 3 (Collins); and *Aen.* VII. 646, Ad nos vix tenuis famae perlabitur aura.

12. Gatty quotes from the *Vision of Sin*:

> All the windy ways of men
> Are but dust that rises up,
> And is lightly laid again.

With which cf. Young, *Night-thoughts*, II. :

> Since by life's passing breath, blown up from Earth,
> Light as the summer's dust, we take in air
> A moment's giddy flight, and fall again.

15. 'credits': perhaps simply 'believes'; but probably rather 'places to the credit of (the doer),' whence comes the further idea of holding in honour.   Cf. LXXX. 13.

20. Cf. *The Dying Swan*, 'the tumult of their acclaim.'

LXXVI.

This section develops the idea expressed in LXXV., stanza 3.   He realises the brevity of any fame which his verses could give to his friend. ' Consider the utter insignificance of the earth and man's life in the universe of worlds ; consider the immeasurable ages of the future ; and then reflect that thy deepest lays will be forgotten in much less than the life-time of a tree on that earth.'

In the *Epilogue* to *The Charge of the Heavy Brigade* the thought of this section is repeated and more clearly expressed :

> The fires that arch this dusky dot—
> Yon myriad-worlded way—

The vast sun-cluster'd gather'd blaze,
  World-isles in lonely skies,
Whole heavens within themselves, amaze
  Our brief humanities ;
And so does Earth ; for Homer's fame,
  Tho' carved in harder stone—
The falling drop will make his name
  As mortal as my own.

The other side is given in *Parnassus* :

If the lips were touch'd with fire from off a pure Pierian
  altar,
Tho' their music here be mortal need the singer greatly
  care ?
Other songs for other worlds ! the fire within him would
  not falter ;
Let the golden Iliad vanish, Homer here is Homer there.

Collins compares with the section Dante, *Purg.*
XI. 91-117, which, he thinks, plainly suggested it
(as well as LXXIII., stanza 3). Cf. also LXXV.
11-13 with lines 92 and 100, 101, of the passage
in Dante.

1. Cf. *Adonais*, XLVII. For the phrase Collins compares
Petrarch, *In Morte*, Sonnet 82, 'Volo con l' ali de' pensieri
al cielo.'

3, 4. 'Where': at a height from which. Gatty compares
Cymbeline, I. iii. 18, 'Till the diminution Of space had
pointed him sharp as my needle.'

6. 'secular' : cf. XLI. 23.

9. 'matin-songs,' etc. : the writings of the great early
Poets (authorised interpretation in Gatty).

11. Cf. 'But Song will vanish in the Vast,' *Epilogue* to
The Charge of the Heavy Brigade.

13. 'these' : yew and oak.

16. Cf. *Merlin and Vivien*, lines 3, 4 :

> Before an oak, so hollow, huge, and old,
> It look'd a tower of ruin'd masonwork.

LXXVII.

Though his songs will soon die, he will sing none the less.   He does not sing for fame.

1-4. The idea (suggested by LXXVI. 1-6) seems to be that, when we look back across the tract of time at objects lying in it, their dimension in the line of vision appears immensely contracted ; and so it will be with modern rhyme.   Cf. *Queen Mary*, III. 5 :

> How many names in the long sweep of time
> That so foreshortens greatness.

For the word 'foreshorten'd' cf. Marvell, *First Anniversary*, 139, 'Foreshortened Time its useless course would stay.' 'Tract of time' occurs in *Par. Lost*, v. 498.

11. 'then changed to something else,' *e.g.* the joy of re-union, in the 'long-forgotten mind.'

13. Cf. XXXVIII. (Eve).

15, 16. Collins compares Petrarch, *In Morte*, Sonnet 25 :

> E certo ogni mio studio in quel temp' era
> > Pur di sfogare il doloroso core
> > In qualche modo, non d' acquistar fama.
> Pianger cercai, non già del pianto onore.

LXXVIII.

With this section begins the Third Part of *In Memoriam*.   See Introduction, p. 29.

The second Christmas-eve after his friend's death.   See XXX. throughout.   There is a great change: the silence and clearness of windless frost instead of the rain, wind, and cloud: a calm and quiet sense of loss, with no outward sign of grief and no pretence of gladness, no 'awful sense of one mute Shadow' and no ecstasy of prophecy. It might almost seem that regret is dead, but in truth it is diffused through the whole substance of life.

5. 'Yule-clog': 'clog'='log' is a dialect-word used in Scotland, some of the northern counties of England, and north Lincolnshire (*Dialect Dictionary*).

11. Tableaux vivants.

12. 'hoodman-blind': blindman's buff. Cf. *Hamlet*, III. iv. 77.

14. 'mark': first ed.: 'type.'

18, 19. 'No': cf. CXV. 18, and contrast Epilogue, 17; 'mystic frame,' 'deep': repeated from XXXVI. 2; 'relations': with everything else in the mystic frame.

SECTIONS LXXIX-LXXXIX.

Many of these eleven sections are occasional poems, having little connection with one another beyond a certain unity of tone. The 'calmness' which is the note of LXXVIII. is maintained. There is much of quiet retrospection, and, in some poems, of thoughts of what might have been: in three sections (LXXXIII., LXXXVI., LXXXVIII.) there is the sense of new life and joy, and the last poem is quite happy. The idea of immortality and the hope of reunion appear but rarely, the centre of interest being shifted to the present life of the poet enriched by love for the dead.

LXXIX.

This section, addressed to one of the poet's brothers, refers back to the last line of IX.

4. 'fee': full possession ; cf. Milton, Sonnet VII. 7, and Wordsworth's Sonnet *On the Extinction of the Venetian Republic*, 'Once did she hold the gorgeous East in fee.'

7 f. Cf. C., CI.

9. Cf. Crabbe, *Delay has Danger* (*Tales*, xiii.) :
> And the cold stream curl'd onward as the gale
> From the pine-hill blew harshly down the dale.

18. Cf. CX. 17.

LXXX.

Here, as in LXXXI. and LXXXIV., the poet is fancying what might have been if his friend had not died. 'If he had lived and I had died, he would have turned his grief into gain. Let his fancied example, then, bring help and comfort to me.'

2, 3. 'holy,' 'kindly.' Contrast his feeling towards the death that took his friend : LXXII., st. 5.

8. 'stay'd': the idea is that the grief is not allowed to separate itself from 'peace with God and man,' but is 'propped' and so held fast in this peace. For the word cf. *Princess*, VII., 'stays all the fair young planet in her hands.'

13. 'His credit': that with which I credit him (in the 'fancy' of 5-12). Cf. LXXI. 5, LXXV. 15. 'Free': suggested by 'burthen': 'help me to turn *my* burthen into gain.'

LXXXI.

' If he had lived, my love for him would have continued to grow.   Yes ; but the same growth was brought suddenly by his death.'

The poem appears at first unintelligible, ' Could I have said ' being naturally read as meaning ' If I could have said,' and ' Love, then, had hope ' as meaning ' Love, then, would have had hope.'   The result is nonsense.

' Could I have said ' is a question.   Accordingly a note of interrogation must be supplied at the end of the first stanza, which should be printed thus :

> Could I have said while he was here,
>   " My love shall now no further range ;
>   There cannot come a mellower change,
> For now is love mature in ear " ?

Line 5 means : '[No, I could not have said this ; and] Love, therefore, had hope of richer store.'   ' But this,' he goes on to say, ' is a painful thought, for it suggests that I have lost the increase of love which would have come if he had lived longer.'   Stanza 3 alludes to the fact that under certain conditions a sudden frost will ripen grain.   The ' grain,' of course, is his love.   Cf. LXV. 4.

The fact that this interpretation of the section involves a change of punctuation need not weigh against it ; for there are frequent instances in *In Memoriam*, and in Tennyson's other works, of defective punctuation, and, in particular, of a defective use of the note of interrogation. For example, LXXXIV. last line, LXXXVII. last line, XCIX. 16, and probably XCIII. 8, should have this note instead of a full stop : in XXXV. 5 and 7 the colon and note should change places. The whole of LXIV. is one interrogative sentence ; it therefore requires a note of interrogation at the end (in addition to a note within the inverted comma). CXIII. 4 should end with a note of exclamation or interrogation. The note in CXIV. 13 should come after 'power' in 15. CXXII. 8 perhaps should have the same note. The note of interrogation has been supplied since the first edition in XXIX. 8, and other places.

For the implied 'no' in line 5 cf. XXIV. 3, and also XCIII. 5, if the sentence is not interrogative.

[I doubt if the interpretation given above is right. It assumes that 'richer store' means 'a store richer than it already was,' or (in other words) 'a store richer than the existing store'; and, with this meaning, it is impossible to take 'could I have said' and 'love had hope' as protasis and apodosis of a conditional sentence. But this is not impossible, if the ellipsis implied in 'richer' is otherwise filled up, and if 'store' is taken to be the grain laid up in garners after Hallam's death. The meaning of lines 1-5, expressed prosaically, will then be : 'If, while he was alive, I had ever been able to say, "My love for him is now fully ripened," I should in that case have been able to anticipate a more valuable store of love, on his death, than the store I could have hoped for on his dying while my love was still unripe.' The full stop after 'ear' in line 4 should then be changed into a comma.

I owe this idea to some remarks by Mr. Ferrall. It avoids the violence to language involved in my interpretation of line 5. I may mention that Tennyson, late in life, endorsed that interpretation, and this of course is a strong argument in its favour ; but I do not consider it decisive.]

LXXXII.

The following summary is intended merely to show the connection with LXXXI. 'Death has not injured my love, which is my best life (LXXXI.) ; nor do I believe he has injured my friend's life. What he has done is to put our lives apart.'

5, 6. Cf. XXX. 25 f., LXI. I. 'From state to state' recurs in *The Two Voices* and in *Demeter and Persephone*, line 7.

7. 'these': the changed 'form and face' of line 2.

10. Did Tennyson know that he was translating Aristotle's χρῆσις τῆς ἀρετῆς ?

11, 12. Cf. LXXIII. 1-4, LXXV. 18-20.

14. 'garners': stores itself. Cf. *Othello*, IV. ii. 57 :

But there where I have garner'd up my heart.

Tennyson's use of the verb as intransitive seems peculiar to him.

15, 16. Cf. LXXXV. 83, 84. Even this complaint is heard no longer towards the close of *In Memoriam*. For the long survival of 'wrath' (which seems somewhat peculiar) cf. LXXII. and XCVIII.

LXXXIII.

The poet calls on the new year to hasten its
coming, to bring the joy and beauty of spring and
summer, and to melt his frozen · sorrow into
song.   The section is, in effect, a spring poem,
and should be contrasted with XXXVIII. and compared with CXV., CXVI.   If he were thinking of
New Year's Day there would be no meaning in
the reference to the 'northern shore' reached by
spring later than southern shores.   Cf. CXVI. 3,
where 'the year' begins in April, and the first
version of *The Miller's Daughter* :

> I heard   .   .   .
> The low voice of the glad New Year
> Call to the freshly flower'd hill.

5. 'from the clouded noons': not 'from bringing the
clouded noons of April,' but, 'from the noons, which are
therefore still clouded.'

6. 'proper': own.   Cf. XXVI. 16, CXVII. 2.

10. The germander speedwell.

11, 12. 'fiery,' 'fire.'   The repetition is, of course, inten-
tional.   Perhaps the famous phrase in 12 suffers from it.
The colour is more truly described in the poem *To Mary
Boyle* :

> And all the gold from each laburnum chain
> Drop to the grass.

('Golden-chain' is a dialect-name for the laburnum-blossom
in the Midlands and South of England.) Mrs. Hemans writes
of the 'laburnum's dropping gold' (G.A.C.).

15. Cf. CXV. 17-20.

LXXXIV.

This section, which deals again with what might have been, is perhaps separated from LXXX. and LXXXI. because it brings no thought of consolation. In spite of some fine phrases it is scarcely in Tennyson's happiest style, and it is unfortunate that the finest lines (19, 20) recall Lamb's exquisite ' Dream Children.' For the biographical references see Introduction, p. 2.

1. 'contemplate': for the accentuation cf. CXVIII. I.

5. 'crown'd': cf. LXXII. 5.

15. G.A.C. quotes Taylor, *Holy Dying*, I. i.: 'and changes his laurel into cypress, his triumphal chariot to an hearse,' and *Romeo and Juliet*, IV. v. 89: 'Our bridal flowers serve for a buried corse.'

41. 'Arrive' is used as sometimes by Shakespeare and Milton.

46. 'backward': retrospective, like Shakespeare's 'record . . . with a backward look' (Sonnet 59).

LXXXV.

The poem is addressed to Edmund Lushington, whose marriage with the poet's sister, Cecilia, is celebrated in the Epilogue (cf. its first line with LXXXV. 5). For the date of composition, see Introduction, p. 14. See also p. 28.

Opening with a repetition, which gives the key-note, of the words which closed XXVII., the poem proceeds to answer the two questions of stanza 3, and so looks both backward and forward, glancing at the moods and subjects of many preceding sections, and showing the stage at which the poet has arrived in his 'progress of sorrow,' and how he seeks a new friendship, though it cannot be like the old.

Collins compares this section with Petrarch's 42nd sonnet ; stanzas 18 and foll. with Sonnet 11 ; and the latter part of the section with Canzone 6. Of the last there seem certainly to be reminiscences, and much of the section is Petrarchian in tone.

21. The pure Spirits, 'whom the vulgar call Angels' (Dante, *Con.* II. 5), who preside over or guide the nine Heavens. Cf. *Parad.* II. 131, XXVIII. 77, and Longfellow's notes. Cf. *Par. Lost*, V. 407, 'those pure intelligential substances,' and VIII. 180. Throughout this section the idea that at death the soul passes into a state which, though higher than the earthly, is still imperfect and gives way to further states, is in abeyance.

22. Cf. *The Princess*, Conclusion : 'That range above the region of the wind.'

28. 'in the cycled times' : in period after period of earthly progress.

33. 'equal-poised' : metaphor from a yoke (Beeching). Cf. *The Princess*, VII., 'yoked in all exercise of noble end.'

35. 'other' : 'second,' which would probably have been written if the lines had not already been full of sibilants, to which Tennyson had an aversion. Cf. *Aen.* VI. 713 : 'animae quibus altera fato Corpora debentur.'

37 f. The sense goes on from line 32 : 'Yet I knew that the will within us (cf. CXXXI.) demands from us action, not absorption in feeling nor works of weakness.' Cf. IV. 15, 16. 'By which,' etc. : through obedience to which we dare to face either life or death. There is no reference to the thought of suicide. Cf. *Essay on Man*, iv. 4 : 'For which we bear to live or dare to die.'

M

43. Cf. LXV. 10.

49. The sense goes on from line 44.

54. 'spiritual strife' : *e.g.* as to immortality or the meaning of evil in the world. Metrically this word is used in three different ways in *In Memoriam* : (1) as here, (2) as in XCII. 14, (3) as in CXXXI. 3.

60. Tennyson seems (*Memoir*, I. 321) to have quoted the words in a way that would identify these 'mighty hopes' with the 'larger hope' of LV. 20. But he may not have had the whole passage in mind ; and, considering the context, it seems more natural to include, at any rate, in the 'mighty hopes' hopes for the future of the race on earth (cf. LXXI. 9-11).

63. Cf. Aug. *Con.* IV. 6 : 'I felt that my soul and his soul were one soul in two bodies, and therefore was my life a horror to me, because I would not live halved' (G.A.C.).

64. 'had' : would have.

67. 'all-assuming' : that take to themselves, devour, everything : Shakespeare's 'Cormorant devouring Time.'

69. 'steaming' : cf. *Par. Lost*, V. 185 :

> 'Ye mists and exhalations that now rise
> From hill or steaming lake.'

'Floods,' rivers : cf. LXXXVI. 7, CIII. 20.

81, 82. Cf. the doubts of XXXVIII., XLIII. foll., LXI. foll. But his resignation in ignorance appears again in 93-6.

85, 86. 'nature' : earthly nature ; 'free' : cf. XXXVIII. 9, 10. I take the stanza to mean, 'Do the dead, then, feel pain (for sympathy must be pain)? Or is their sympathy painless?' But it has been pointed out to me that the idea of the last two lines need not be an alternative to that of the first, the meaning of the stanza being : 'Can the life of the dead be clouded by sympathy, doubtless painless, with the living?' In either case the stanza touches on a difficulty as to memory in the dead which has not previously been alluded to.

90. Cf. LXIX. 20.

91. 'conclusive' : the bliss of the 'final goal' (LIV. 2) or

'divine event.' The dead friend is supposed to see, where the poet can only trust. Cf. CXXVII. 20.

95. 'symbols': thoughts which signify figuratively a truth which they do not accurately express.

101. 'If, with love as true, if not so fresh, I,' etc. 'If' is forced ungrammatically to do double duty. [But this would be a strange mistake, and Mr. Ferrall is probably right in taking the sentence to be independent of the preceding stanza : 'with love as true, if not so fresh (as my first love for my dead friend), I aver,' etc.]

105. 'apart': in a place which no other 'powers' can occupy.

106. 'golden hours': cf. XXXIX. 6.

107. Cf. VI. 43, 44, and 'deep as first love' in *Tears, idle Tears*.

112. Cf. VII. 3, 4.

113. 'widow'd': cf. IX. 18.

119. The Evening Primrose, according to many readers ; but surely Tennyson meant the feeble or imperfect flowers sometimes put forth by the common primrose in autumn and early winter.

LXXXVI.

This wonderful poem, written in spring (6, 10) 'at Barmouth,' famed for the sunsets over its estuary, 'gives pre-eminently his sense of the joyous peace in Nature, and he would quote it in this context along with his Spring and Bird songs' (*Memoir*, I. 313). It is the answer to the prayer of LXXXIII., and comes most appropriately at this point, breathing the 'full new life' which is beginning to revive in the poet's heart, and to dispel the last shadow of the evil dreams which Nature seemed to lend (LV.) when he was under the sway of the ill brethren Doubt and Death. The rhythm of the one long sentence, the pauses of which are not allowed to coincide with the breaks between the stanzas, seems the very echo of the spirit of the poem. See further, on this section, the remarks on CXXII.; and cf. with it a passage at the beginning of *The Lover's Tale*, III.:

> A morning air, sweet after rain, ran over
> The rippling levels of the lake, and blew
> Coolness and moisture and all smells of bud
> And foliage from the dark and dripping woods
> Upon my fever'd brows that shook and throbb'd
> From temple unto temple.

For the date of composition see p. 15.

1. 'ambrosial': a favourite word with Milton and Tenny-son, who uses 'ambrosial gloom' in a very early fragment (*Memoir*, I. 24), and again in *The Princess*, IV. 6.

3, 4. Cf. CXXII. 4.

5. 'rapt': the word does not imply quick or violent motion with Tennyson. Cf. *The Day-dream*:

> And, rapt thro' many a rosy change,
> The twilight died into the dark.

6. 'dewy': from the showers. Ct. CII. 12, and *The Princess*, I.: 'In the green gleam of dewy-tassell'd trees.'

7. 'shadowing': cf. CVII. 14, and 'Little breezes dusk and shiver,' *Lady of Shalott*. 'Horned flood': see on LXXXV. 69. 'Horned' probably means not 'branching' but 'wind-ing,' and so 'indented.' Cf. *The Dying Swan*, 'And the wave-worn horns of the echoing bank.' Cf. 'horned flood' in *Par. Lost*, XI. 831, and Virgil's 'Corniger Hesperidum fluvius regnator aquarum,' *Aen.* VIII. 77.

13 ff. 'The west wind rolling to the Eastern seas till it meets the evening star': Tennyson's words to Mr. Knowles. I had always taken the lines to mean that fancy accom-

panies the west wind as it streams eastward from cloud-belt to cloud-belt in the crimson *sky*, or from belt to belt of crimson *cloud*. Such uses of 'sea' are, of course, common, and cf. LXXXIX. 47, CIII. 55, *The Ancient Sage*,

> The last long stripe of waning crimson gloom.

I cannot help suspecting some misunderstanding on Mr. Knowles's part, or even a forgetfulness of his meaning on Tennyson's, not so much because it is hard to imagine what 'Eastern seas,' except the Red, would look from above like 'belts,' as because any Eastern sea would be dark when sunset was visible from the west of England, a fact which Tennyson would be the last poet to forget.

With the whole stanza cf. the last stanza of the Alcaics to Milton.

14. 'odour': caught from 'brake and bloom and meadow' and 'dewy-tassell'd wood.' Cf. XCV. 9.

LXXXVII.

A retrospect of Cambridge days, not marked by the sense of loss. See p. 16.

6. 'high-built,' in reference to the position of the organ above the screen (Gatty).

7. Cf. a fine description at the end of *The Princess*, II.

8. 'prophet': first ed.: 'prophets.' The change was not made till 1884.

15. 'long walk of limes,' in Trinity College. Cf. Sonnet *To the Rev. W. H. Brookfield*:

> How oft with him we paced that walk of limes,
> Him, the lost light of those dawn-golden times.

39, 40. 'These lines I wrote from what Arthur Hallam said after reading of the prominent ridge of bone over the eyes of Michael Angelo: "Alfred, look over my eyes; surely I have the bar of Michael Angelo!"' Tennyson, quoted in *Memoir*, I. 38.

LXXXVIII.

As in the bird's song, so in his own, joy
seems to break from the midst of grief.

1. The 'wild bird' is generally and naturally taken to be
the nightingale, whose song seems to some 'most melancholy,' and to others joyous, and to the poet both. Cf. a
passage near the end of the *Gardener's Daughter*, and, earlier,
Recollections of the Arabian Nights:

> The living airs of middle night
> Died round the bulbul as he sung ;
> Not he : but something which possess'd
> The darkness of the world, delight,
> Life, anguish, death, immortal love,
> Ceasing not, mingled, unrepress'd.

Tennyson elsewhere uses both 'warble' and 'liquid' of the
nightingale's song.

2. 'quicks': the quick-set hedge-row : cf. CXV. 2. The
word is used by country folk in various parts of England.

3 f. What is that centre where the diverse passions so
mingle that, when they radiate from it, each has a tone of
the others ?

5. 'fierce extremes': occurs in *King John*, V. vii. 13 ;
Par. Lost, VII. 272.

6. 'darkening,' as night comes on : first ed. : 'dusking,'
often used by Tennyson of twilight. The change was
perhaps made because of 'dusk' in LXXXIX. 2.

11. 'the sum of things': occurs in *Par. Lost*, VI. 673
(G.A.C.).

LXXXIX.

An entirely happy retrospect of his friend's
visits to the poet's home. For the biographical
references see pp. 2, 3. It will be found that (if
we omit the long section LXXXV.) sections of

LXXXVIII.,LXXXIX. Commentary 183

hope and of retrospect are made to alternate in this part of the poem: LXXXIII., LXXXVI., LXXXVIII., with LXXXIV., LXXXVII., LXXXIX.

1. 'counterchange': chequer. Cf. LXXII. 15, and *Recollections of the Arabian Nights*:

> A sudden splendour from behind
> Flushed all the leaves with rich gold-green,
> And, flowing rapidly between
> Their interspaces, counterchanged
> The level lake with diamond-plots
> Of dark and bright.

4. 'sycamore': cf. XCV. 55.

7. 'liberal air': cf. Byron, *Manfred*, I. 1, 'pipes in the liberal air.'

8. Cf. Horace, Odes, III. xxix. 12, 'Fumum et opes strepitumque Romae' (Collins).

12. 'dusty': first ed. : 'dusky.'

16. 'winking' of course refers to the tremulous appearance of the heated air.

27. G.A.C. compares Hallam's *Remains*, p. 71 :

> Sometimes I dream thee leaning o'er
> The harp I used to love so well.

36. Arthur Hallam was an enthusiastic reader of Plato.

45. 'glooming': Tennyson is fond of 'gloom' and its congeners. He uses 'glooming' as a substantive in the *Gardener's Daughter* ('the balmy glooming crescent-lit'; cf. 'gorgeous gloom of evening,' LXXXVI. 2), and 'gloom' as a transitive verb in *The Letters* and elsewhere. Cf. Epilogue, 118. Cf. with the whole line Horace, Odes, II. xi. 18 (G.A.C.).

47, 48. These lines, which surely mar a beautiful passage, mean : 'Before Venus, surrounded by the crimson of sunset, had set after the sun.' Cf. CXXI. 1, 2. According to the nebular theory, Venus, like the other planets, was formed by the condensation of a zone thrown off from a mass of nebula, the remains of which, condensing towards the centre, formed the sun. The sun, as representing the whole original nebula, is figured as the father of Venus. Cf. Lady Psyche in *The Princess*, II. :

> This world was once a fluid haze of light,
> Till toward the centre set the starry tides,
> And eddied into suns, that wheeling cast
> The planets.

'crimson-circled': for 'crimson' cf. CIII. 55 (of cloud), and perhaps LXXXVI. 13.

52. Cf. CI. 8.

SECTIONS XC.-XCV.

A group of closely connected sections on the present communion or contact of the living and the dead. It opens with the expression of desire for such communion, and closes with the description of an experience in which this desire seems to be fulfilled.

So far the thought of such present communion has occupied the poet but little. He trusts to meet his friend beyond the grave ; he has hoped that his friend watches him from afar ; he has even cried to him ' Be near me.' But he has accepted the fact of their present separation, and the one deed for which he has been unable to forgive Death is that

> He put our lives so far apart
> We cannot hear each other speak (LXXXII.).

Now, with the desire for communion, comes the thought that after all it may in some form be possible even in this life. The connection of the sections is shown in the summaries which follow.

XC.

'Come back to me!' The idea is quite general : he does not ask in what way his friend is to return to him.

1. He who first suggested the ideas expressed in stanzas 2-5 never loved with all his soul, and never knew love at its highest. With these stanzas cf. *The Lotos-Eaters*, VI., where the phrase 'confusion worse than death' recurs.

15, 16. G.A.C. quotes from Sadi's *Gulistan* : 'Oh ! if the dead man might come again among the members of his race and his kindred, the return of his inheritance would be harder to the heir than the death of his relation.'

17. 'these': the sons mentioned in stanzas 2, 3, 4.

22. See Introduction, p. 17.

XCI.

'Come back to me in visible form !' The *visible form* is the 'point' of the section. He calls on his friend to appear ; in spring-time, wearing the semblance worn in the spring-tide promise of his life on earth (1-8) ; in summer, in the 'after form' which betokens his maturer life elsewhere (9-16). (Genung alone among the analysts has perceived the structure of the poem, and the beauty of the descriptive phrases probably conceals it from many readers.)

2. 'rarely.' The 'rarely' of Shakespeare and of Scott's
> Sweet Robin sits on the bush,
> Singing so rarely.

4. 'sea-blue bird of March': the kingfisher. Cf. *The Progress of Spring* :
> And in her open palm a halcyon sits
> Patient—the secret splendour of the brooks.

The phrase is fully explained in the following passage : ' As
to " sea-blue birds " &c. defendant states that he was walking
one day in March by a deep-banked brook, and under the
leafless bushes he saw the kingfisher flitting or fleeting
underneath him, and there came into his head a fragment of
an old Greek lyric poet [Alkman], " ἀλιπόρφυρος εἴαρος ὄρνις,"
" The sea-purple or sea-shining bird of Spring," spoken of as
the halcyon.   Defendant cannot say whether the Greek
halcyon be the same as the British kingfisher, but, as he
never saw the kingfisher on this particular brook before
March, he concludes that in that country, at least, they go
down to the sea during the hard weather, and come up again
with the Spring, for what says old Belon :

> " Le Martinet-pescheur fait sa demeure
> En temps d'hiver au bord de l'océan,
> Et en esté sur la rivière en estan,
> Et de poisson se repaist à toute heure."

You see he puts " esté," which I suppose stands for all the
warmer weather.'   Letter of Tennyson to Duke of Argyll,
1864, *Memoir*, II. 4.   The letter is perfectly decisive, yet by
1890 these details had faded from Tennyson's mind, and,
though he 'supposed' the bird was the kingfisher, he was
willing to believe it was the blue tit (see Rawnsley's *Memories
of the Tennysons*, p. 109).

6. 'in time': in the earthly life.   Cf. XXVII. 6.

16. 'light in light.'   Cf. ' another night in night,' *Recollections of the Arabian Nights*.

XCII.

' No : it is no visible appearance that I desire,
nor any communication through sense.   I should
not be convinced.'   Reflection destroys the wish
expressed in XCI.   For, if the vision came, it
might be counted a mere hallucination.   Even if

it spoke, and spoke of events in the lives of the
friends on earth, this might be counted the product of his own memory.   Nay, if it foretold
something which actually happened a year later,
the prophecy might seem to be merely his own
presentiment.   Contrast this section with XIV.

3. Cf. *Maud*, II. iv. 8 :

> Get thee hence, nor come again,
> Mix not memory with doubt.

> *   *   *

> 'Tis the blot upon the brain
> That *will* show itself without.

13. 'They' seems to have nothing to refer to except
'months.' But, probably, as several correspondents suggest,
the sense is, ' It might not seem thy prophecy,' but Tennyson,
writing 'prophecies,' put 'they' by a kind of attraction from
that plural.   The line is thus equivalent to, ' Thy prophecies
might not seem thy prophecies.'

14. 'spiritual': 'in my own spirit,' or, 'such as often come
into the mind' (Ferrall).

15, 16 do not give another hypothesis, but repeat 14 (he
says 'And,' not 'Or'). 'Refraction,' as in mirage. Gatty
quotes from Coleridge's translation of the *Death of Wallen-
stein*, V. i.:

> As the sun,
> Ere it is risen, sometimes paints its image
> In the atmosphere, so often do the spirits
> Of great events stride on before the events,
> And in to-day already walks to-morrow.

The context makes it probable that there is here a reminiscence of this passage.   Cf. Coleridge's *Statesman's Manual*,
Appendix B, and *Table Talk*, May 1, 1823 (G.A.C.).

XCIII.

' But a direct contact of soul and soul is possible. Therefore come ! '

1-4. 'See' is emphatic. Understand 'But' before 'Dare,' or 'then' after 'Dare I.' The poet abruptly and finally dismisses the idea that the dead will appear in visible form, but hesitates to assert that no soul ever returned to earth.

5-8. He affirms that it is possible that the soul of the dead—not a visual shade, but the soul itself—may come to the soul of the living without the mediation of any sense, or on condition that all the senses are in abeyance ('all' in 7 excludes more than the 'see' of 1, unless the line means, 'When the nerve of sight is wholly numb,' when cf. *Par. Lost*, XI. 415, 'the visual nerve'). Such words as 'No, I dare not say this. Rather' must be understood before the beginning of line 5. Cf. the omission of 'No, I could not have said this' in LXXXI. 5 (on one interpretation).

But the passage from doubt or musing ('Dare I say?') to positive assertion is here so abrupt that perhaps stanza 2 was really meant to be a continuation of lines 2-4 of stanza 1 ; *i.e.* to be a part of that which the poet doubts whether he dare say : 'dare I say, not indeed that the visual shade may come, but that the spirit himself may come?' In that case, line 4 should end with a colon or semi-colon, and line 8 with a note of interrogation. On Tennyson's defective use of this note, see remarks on LXXXI. If this suggestion be correct, the summary given at the head of the section will run : 'But is not a direct contact of soul and soul possible? If so, come !'

A third interpretation has been suggested to me as conceivable : 'I shall not see thee. No spirit (dare I say this?) ever came back to the world of sense : none ever appeared as a shade : but a spirit may return to the inner world of another spirit.'

8. Cf. *Aylmer's Field* :

> Star to star vibrates light : may soul to soul
> Strike thro' a finer element of her own ?
> So,—from afar,—touch us at once?

These lines, however, refer to two living people, one at the point of death. (In the lines that follow there is another instance of the omission of the note of interrogation).

9. 'thy sightless range' : the place where thou rangest invisible. For 'range' cf. XLIV. 12, LXXXV. 22 : for 'sightless' (used as in *Macbeth*, I. v. 50, vii. 23) CXV. 18.

10. Cf. *Comus*, 11.

13. Cf. CXXII. 11.

15. 'frame'; body, as in XLV. 11 (but not as in XXXVI. 2). Cf. 7.

XCIV.

He reflects, and realizes what is required in his own soul for such communion. Cf. the way in which LI., LII. follow on L. Cf. Taylor's *Twenty-five Sermons preached at Golden Grove*, Sermon iv. (Collins).

6. shows a curious coincidence with a line in Young's *Night-thoughts*, IV. :

> To drink the spirit of the golden day.

10. (They haunt) imaginations.

14. 'doubt' : see XCV. 44. If this connection was intended (which seems very questionable) the doubt in XCV. was regarded as blameable.

15. 'gates' : cf. 'enter,' XCIII. 13.

16. For the metaphors of this stanza cf. Herbert, *The Family*.

XCV.

After a peaceful evening in the garden formerly visited by his friend, the poet, left alone in the

summer night, reads again the letters of the
dead, and suddenly his wish is, in some sense,
fulfilled.

For the 'trance,' and Tennyson's own experiences and opinions, see Introduction, pp. 46, 53,
60 ; the passages quoted in the note on line
39 ; *Memoir*, I. 320, 321, and Mr. Knowles's
article, p. 169.   Tennyson's experience seems to
have resembled that of Plotinus (see *Enn.* IV.
viii. 1).

On this section see further the notes on CXXII.

1. The scene of LXXXIX., and therefore the happy memories
of the past, are recalled by the opening reference to the
lawn, and the later mention of the brook, the sycamore,
and the elms.

9. 'fragrant': cf. LXXXVI. 14.

10. 'lit': alighted ; 'the filmy shapes,' etc. : night-moths
(authorised interpretation in Gatty, who adds that the
ermine moth answers to the description).

22. 'that glad year,' as the metaphor of the next line
shows, is the whole time of the friendship.

25 f. The strangeness of the dead man's seeming to be
then and there speaking, expressed in 'silent-speaking' and
'dumb cry,' prepares for what follows.

34. 'touch'd': the word was used in XCIII. 13.

36, 37. 'The living soul,' 'And mine in this': till about
1878, 'His living soul,' 'And mine in his.'   On 'the
living soul' Tennyson remarked to Mr. Knowles : 'perchance of the Deity. . . .   My conscience was troubled by
"his." ' [1]

[1] What was it that troubled his conscience? A doubt whether it
had really *seemed* to him that Hallam's soul was flashed on his ?
Rather, I suppose, a doubt whether the soul that seemed to be
flashed on his, and seemed to be Hallam's, *was* Hallam's.   If so,

'living,' in antithesis to 'dead' (34). 'Flash'd,' to describe instantaneous motion or action. Cf. XLI. 12, LXXVI. 5.

39. 'that which is': the ultimate reality, as distinguished from that half-deceptive appearance which we commonly call the real world. Cf. CXXIV. 22 ; *The Higher Pantheism* ; the grand conclusion of the *Holy Grail*, where 'vision' (appearance) is distinguished from reality ; and especially the *Ancient Sage*.

41. He is able to perceive the law and harmony in what at other times appears unintelligible ; cf. CXXII. 8. 'Aeonian': cf. XXXV. 11.

42, 43. Cf. Milton, *On Time*, 'Triumphing over Death and Chance and thee, O Time.'

45-8. 'My description of that which I became during the trance and in its cancelling is vague ; but how can it be otherwise ?' It might seem at first more natural to take 'that which I became' to refer to the time *after* the cancelling of the trance. In that case the meaning of the stanza will be : My description of the trance and its cancelling is vague, but to describe the state that followed would be even more difficult. Accordingly he does not attempt to describe it. But is it likely that his state, after the trance was cancelled by doubt, would be even further removed from ordinary experience than his state during the trance ?

'matter-moulded': the forms of speech, being moulded by and meant to express our sensible experience, are inadequate to describe a higher experience. Such words, for example, as 'Descend, and touch, and enter' (XCIII. 13),

his scruple seems needless, for he had never said that it *was* Hallam's (see 35) ; he had said that his trance was cancelled by doubt (44) ; and, if he referred to it in CXXII., he had again spoken doubtfully of Hallam's presence. Probably at the moment of the experience he did think his friend's soul was present, but thereafter never felt any certainty on the subject ; and, considering the language of such a poem as CXXX., his uncertainty seems almost inevitable.

properly apply to something material, and not to the soul. And equally inadequate will be the language which describes the trance.

Collins compares with the stanza *Paradiso*, XXXIII. 55-7.

49. 'doubtful': cf. LXI. 9. The last four stanzas form surely, if taken alone, one of the most wonderful descriptive passages in all poetry ; but in their context they have an indescribable effect, the breeze seeming to recall the coming and passing of the wind of the Spirit in the trance, and the mingling of the dim lights of East and West being seen as that meeting of life and death which has just been experienced as the precursor of an endless union to come.

63. Cf. Herbert, *The Search.* Cf. *The Ring*,

> And past and future mix'd in Heaven, and made
> The rosy twilight of a perfect day.

'Dim lights of life' occurs in Pope's *Elegy to the Memory*, etc., 19.

XCVI.

This section has no connection with the preceding group, unless through the mention of 'doubt' in XCIV. 14, and XCV. 30, 44. Line 11 however at once recalls XCV. 29, 30 ; and hence it seems not unlikely that in XCVI. also the poet is describing his friend. It is true, as Genung observes, that neither the lines in XCV. nor CIX. 6 imply that Hallam had to 'fight his doubts.' But a sonnet by Hallam, printed in the *Remains*, p. 75, refers to a period when doubt 'made an unkind December of [his] spring' ; and cf. the Preface to the *Remains*, p. xxxi.

Mr. Ferrall thinks the poet is referring to himself, and to that conquest over doubt on which the experience described in XCV. has set the seal.

The interest of this question is merely bio-graphical, and the reference need not be either to Tennyson or to Hallam. With the section cf. XXXIII.

18 foll. : cf. CXXIV. 2, 4, 23.

22 f. The same passages from *Exodus*, xix. and xxxii. are referred to in a poem of doubtful authorship in *Poems by Two Brothers*. The last two lines seem chiefly intended to complete the picture of the scene suggested by 21, 22, without much regard to their bearing on the main subject of the section : for if anything now corresponds to the trumpet then, there would seem to be no more excuse for doubt now than for turning to strange gods then. This addition of almost irrelevant details in a simile is classical. Cf. for it the last two lines of ' Clear-headed friend.' It may be, how-ever, as has been suggested to me, that the ' cloud' answers to intellectual uncertainty, the ' trumpet' to the feelings so often referred to as giving what intellect cannot give, and the ' making of gods of gold' to that misconduct into which the doubter did not fall, though he was perplext in faith (see line 9).

XCVII.

This section recalls LX. See note on the group which opens with that section. The short, simple, unconnected sentences recall the style of LXIX.

1 ff. The first stanza is prefatory. The poet's love finds an echo of itself in the common things of nature (1), in her more mystical appearances (2, 3), in fact everywhere (4), and so in ' two partners of a married life ' (5). Cf. LXXXV. 69-76. For ' he' cf. CXXVIII. 2. The preface, however, seems too fine for what follows, the style of the rest of the poem being some-what plain for Tennyson, though in harmony with the substance.

N

2, 3. The allusion is to the spectre of the Brocken. [A correspondence in the *Spectator* for Sept. 21 and 28, 1901, shows the necessity of explaining that the 'spectre' is the observer's shadow thrown on a bank of mist. If the bank is near him his shadow may appear enormously extended and, so, 'vast.' He sees a halo round its head, but not round the head of any fellow-observer's shadow.]

7. Cf. 3.

15. 'earnest': pledge.

16. Cf. LX. 13, 14.

21. Cf. Pope, *Rape of the Lock*, II. 139, 'Some thrid the mazy ringlets of her hair'; and *The Princess*, IV., 'to thrid the musky-circled mazes.'

XCVIII.

To friends about to visit Vienna, where Hallam died. The feeling of reconciliation with death is disturbed. For the occasion and date of the section see Introduction, p. 15.

3. 'When I was there with him': in July, 1832.

7, 8. 'wisp': Will o' the wisp; 'in the eyes of': watched by.

11. The author kept his word.

17. 'gnarr': snarl. Cf. Spenser, *F.Q.*, I. v. 34, 'felly gnarre' (of Cerberus), and Shakespeare's 'gnarl': 'For gnarling sorrow hath less power to bite,' *R. II.*, I. iii. 292.

25. 'mother town': metropolis.

XCIX.

The second anniversary of his friend's death: Sept. 15. The poem opens with the same words as LXXII., to which it forms a beautiful contrast.

5. 'Darkling red' probably describes the fading of rosy clouds towards blackness, not the deepening redness of a clear sky. Such fading is a sign of coming rain. Cf.

'dimly' (1), 'swollen' (6). Most readers seem to imagine a morning sunny as well as calm and soft, but there is nothing to indicate the former.

9. 'foliaged': the word 'murmurest' suggests the foliage of trees, so that 'foliaged' may mean 'overshadowed by leafy trees': but it is more likely that it is used as in *Alastor*, 'foliaged lattice.' Cf. *L'Allegro* :

> And at my window bid good morrow,
> Through the sweet-briar or the vine
> Or the twisted eglantine.

Mr. Ferrall, to whom I owe the observation about 'murmurest,' suggests that 'foliaged eaves' may even mean 'eaves of foliage,' the foliage being that of trees overshadowing the lawn. And I have seen 'eaves' so used in poetry.

12. 'fiery': cf. CI. 4.

13-20. Contrast VI., st. 2. The expansion of feeling here prepares us for the poems about to follow.

13. 'balmy breath': cf. *Othello*, v. ii. 16: 'Ah, balmy breath, that dost almost persuade Justice to break her sword.'

17. 'those' of 16.

18. Cf. 'All things that move between the quiet poles,' Marlowe, *Dr. Faustus*, opening soliloquy.

SECTIONS C.-CIII.

The poet leaves the home which has so many associations both with his childhood and with his friend. Loving retrospect is mingled with the impulse forwards to a larger life. This group forms a transition to the last Part of *In Memoriam*. The reader has been prepared for it by the descriptions in LXXIX, LXXXIX, XCV., and XCIX., so that he seems to be familiar with the home that has to be left.

For the occasion and date see Introduction, p. 15.

C.

In leaving the old home he seems to lose his friend again ; but the original feeling of loss is reproduced faintly and peacefully, and the memories recalled are not poignant but 'gracious' and tender.

1. 'I climb the hill': first ed.: 'I wake, I rise': which failed to indicate the point of view. For 'the hill' cf. LXXXIX. 30.

9, 10. The time is autumn, between the times of XCIX. and CIV.

13. Cf. 'the tinkling rills,' Pope, *Eloisa to Abelard*, 158, and Marvell, *Clorinda and Damon*,

> Near this, a fountain's liquid bell
> Tinkles within the concave shell.

17. Cf. VIII. 21.

CI.

He turns, in this exquisite poem, from the associations of the home with his friend to its associations with his own childhood.

3. 'beech': cf. XXX. 9.

4. Cf. II. 11, XCIX. 12.

8. Cf. LXXXIX. 52.

9 f. The brook seems to have been an object of special affection. Cf. LXXIX. 9, 10, LXXXIX. 43-5, XCV. 7, XCIX. 5, 6, C. 14-16. The present lines seem to be the germ of *The Brook*.

11, 12. 'or when,' etc. The pole-star, one of the stars in the 'lesser wain,' or *ursa minor*, forms the apparent axis of that constellation. The periphrasis seems needlessly elaborate, but it presumably recalls the boy's pleasure in watching this constellation, with the sound of the unseen brook coming to him from time to time.   Collins quotes Sophocles, *Trach.* 130, ἄρκτου στροφάδες κέλευθοι.   Cf. *Lay of the Last Minstrel*, I. xvii.:

> Arthur's slow wain his course doth roll,
> In utter darkness, round the pole.

15. Cf. XLIX. 3, 4.

18. 'blow,' like a flower.

21. 'the labourer,' who does not move away, but belongs to the landscape.

CII.

Love for the home of childhood (CI.), and love for the home associated with the dead (C.), are beautifully figured as rivals in a game in which both must lose.   As he goes, they unite.

Cf. Petrarch, *In Vita*, Sonnet XLIV. (Collins).

1-4. The reader will recall a famous passage in Cowper's lines *On the Receipt of my Mother's Picture*, but Tennyson owes nothing to it.

7, 8. 'referring to the double loss of his father and of his friend' (*Memoir*, I. 72): but of course this does not imply that the one 'spirit' is his father and the other his friend ; and indeed no one could have guessed from the poem that there was any reference to the former.   See CV. 5.

12. 'tassel-hung': cf. LXXXVI. 6.

19. G. A. C. compares *Queen Mab*, iii. :

> for kings
> And subjects, mutual foes, for ever play
> A losing game into each other's hands.

22. Cf. Virgil, *Ecl.* I. 3 : 'Nos patriae fines et dulcia linquimus arva.'

24. Perhaps the idea is that it is the pain of regret that unites them.

CIII.

His sadness at leaving the old home is changed to content by a dream. In interpreting this dream we must remember that, even if its record is affected by waking imagination, it is not likely to form an entirely consistent allegory, and also that the dream, though primarily about the poet's life, is also about human life in general. The river fed from hidden summits is life on earth. The sea is eternity, or the life beyond (this image is habitual with Tennyson: cf. CXXV. 13; *The Passing of Arthur*, where the 'great water' opens on the Ocean; the passing of Galahad in *The Holy Grail*; *Crossing the Bar*). The maidens, Tennyson believed (Gatty), stand for 'the Muses, Arts, etc.'; but, in so far as the dream concerns the individual life of the poet, they must rather stand for the corresponding aspirations and activities within him; especially for his poetry, and, perhaps, eminently the poems about his friend; otherwise their growing and departing with him would be meaningless. They sing to the statue, for the poet's friend is both the centre of his love and a type to him (see the coming sections) of the ideal humanity of the future, already realised in the other life. Their ignorance (12, 13), their wailing (18), and their reproaches (45-48), appear to indicate that, though aspiring to the ideal, they recognise it only in its earthly forms, and so take the poet's departure to be a desertion of these forms and of them. Their

passing with him to the other life means that
'everything that made Life beautiful here, we
may hope may pass on with us beyond the
grave' (authorised interpretation in Gatty).
Stanzas 7-9 typify the broadening and deepening
of life, and the spiritual expansion which will fit
the poet to meet his friend again ; also 'the great
progress of the age' (Tennyson to Mr. Knowles).

The growth of love for the friend into love
for mankind—or, rather, for the divine humanity
to which mankind is advancing—is seen in this
section, and becomes prominent later.

5, 6. Cf. the 'mystic mountain-range' in *The Vision of Sin*,
and *The Ancient Sage* :

> This wealth of waters might but seem to draw
> From yon dark cave, but, son, the source is higher,
> Yon summit half-a-league in air—and higher,
> The cloud that hides it—higher still, the heavens
> Whereby the cloud was moulded, and whereout
> The cloud descended. Force is from the heights.

Cf. also *The Poet's Mind.*

8. Cf. *Geor.* II. 157, 'Fluminaque antiquos subterlabentia
muros.'

14, 15. 'I loved, and love For ever.'   The words are
almost repeated in the last line of *Vastness.*

20. 'flood': river : cf. LXXXVI. 7.

24. 'golden reed'; this does not appear to be the popular
name of any plant. The Branched Bur-reed, *Sparganium
Ramosum*, seems most likely to be the plant intended. It
has been suggested that 'iris' means the purple iris, and
'golden reed' the yellow one, but the purple one does not
grow in the situation required.

30. Cf. Epilogue, 19, 20.

33-36. For this 'Vision of the World' cf. CXVIII. 14, Epilogue, 128 ff., *Locksley Hall, Locksley Hall Sixty Years After*.

SECTIONS CIV.-CVI.

With these sections begins the Fourth Part of *In Memoriam*. See p. 34.

Christmastide and New Year in the new home. The poet turns away from the past and its private grief, and looks to the future and his hopes for mankind.

This is the third Christmas since his friend's death. See XXVIII.-XXX., LXXVIII. For the localities and date see Introduction, p. 15. The church of CIV. 3 is Waltham Abbey.

CIV.

1, 2. Repeated from XXVIII. 1, 2. The remainder of the section forms a detailed contrast with XXVIII.

11. 'breathes': a favourite word with Tennyson as with Milton. Cf. (in this part of the poem) XCIX. 7, C. 3.

12. 'unhallow'd': contrast XCIX. 8.

CV.

Christmas Eve.   See XXIX., XXX., and LXXVIII.

1, 2. First ed. :

> This holly by the cottage eave,
>   To night, ungather'd, shall it stand.

The change was probably made because 'eave' and 'eve' do not rhyme. Yet see on VIII. 5, 8.

4. 'strangely': contrast 'sadly,' XXX. 4, and 'calmly,' LXXVIII. 4.

6. There is a reminiscence, perhaps unconscious, of LXXVIII. 3.

7, 8. Cf. Moschus, Idyll III. 100.

9. 'abuse': in the old sense of 'wrong.' Cf. XXX. 6.

10. Cf. LXXVIII. 11 foll.

12. 'use': cf. XXIX. 11.

14. 'proved': tried.

17. 'beat': in dancing: cf. I. 12.

24. 'what,' etc.: 'such motion of rising stars as lightens,' etc. The idea of the stars dancing is common in Milton; *e.g. Par. Lost*, III. 580, V. 178. 'East': cf. XXX. 29-32 (Robinson).

27. 'Complete the allotted number of your revolutions.' Cf. CXVII. 12.

28. 'the closing cycle' or period: cf. CIII. 35, CVI. 28, Epilogue, 128 ff. Tennyson uses the language of the Roman poets, *e.g.* Horace in the *Carmen Saeculare*, or Virgil, *Ecl.* IV. 4, *Ultima* Cymaei venit jam carminis *aetas*. Time is said to have been divided in the books of the Cumaean Sybil into cycles or saecula, and Virgil makes the golden age return with the closing cycle.

CVI.

New Year's Eve. The mood of the last poem is continued and heightened; the bells sound wild and jubilant, as though the 'closing cycle' were already beginning; and the poet turns from 'the grief that saps the mind' to hopes for the future of man.

In this section it should be observed that the powers that work for good are especially those which unite men; and so the feeling that his grief isolates him and is useless to others stirs the poet to overcome it (CVIII.).

9, 10, 19, 20.   Cf. Prologue, 37 ff., LXXXV. 61, 62, and Epilogue, 21 ff.

12. Cf. Prologue, 12.

27. Cf. CIII. 33.

32. 'My father expressed his conviction . . . that the forms of Christian religion would alter, but that the spirit of Christ would still grow from more to more "in the roll of the ages,"

> Till each man find his own in all men's good,
> And all men work in noble brotherhood.

"This is one of my meanings," he said, "of

> Ring in the Christ that is to be :

when Christianity without bigotry will triumph, when the controversies of creeds shall have vanished, and

> Shall bear false witness, each of each, no more,
> But find their limits by that larger light,
> And overstep them, moving easily
> Thro' after-ages in the Love of Truth,
> The Truth of Love."' (*Memoir*, I. 325, 6).

For the antithesis with 'the *darkness* of the land' cf. XXX. 29-32.

CVII.

The friend's birthday (Feb. 1) shall be kept cheerily, as though he himself were there.

The change in the poet's attitude, seen in his dismissal both of grief and of speculation about the dead, is strongly marked.

In writing this section, Tennyson doubtless remembered not only Horace, *Odes*, I. ix., but the fragment of Alcaeus on which that Ode is based.

8. Cf. *The Progress of Spring* :

> from all the dripping eaves
> The spear of ice has wept itself away.

'sharpen'd' : by the ice on them.

9. The icy bushes and thorns point like bristles towards the moon. Cf. *Walking to the Mail* :

> There by the hump-back'd willow : half stands up
> And bristles.

11. 'grides . . . together': makes grate together. ' Gride ' originally meant 'pierce,' without any reference to sound, and there does not appear to be any such reference in Spenser's or Milton's use of the word (*e.g. P.L.*, VI. 329). It is probable that Tennyson was influenced by Shelley, *Prom. Unb.*, III. i. :

> Hear ye the thunder of the fiery wheels
> Griding the winds?

for he uses the word of thunder in ' The heavy thunder's griding might,' *Chorus* in *Poems* (1830).

'clangs . . . together ': cf. *Boadicea* :

Till her people all around the royal chariot agitated,
Madly dash'd the darts together, writhing barbarous linea-
    ments,
Made the noise of frosty woodlands, when they shiver in
    January.

12 'iron' may refer to sound as well as to the stiffness of the ascending branches.

13, 14. 'drifts ': Gatty says, ' drifts of snow, which falling into water immediately blacken before they dissolve,' and readers seem usually to take the passage thus. But it is difficult to reconcile this interpretation with the ' purple-frosty bank,' ' bristles,' the ' hard crescent,' and the sounds of the wood : and it seems more likely that the drifts are violent squalls of *wind* (cf. 6, 7) which are seen to strike and darken the moon-lit rollers (cf. LXXXVI. 7). The only objection to this is that Tennyson apparently does not elsewhere use ' drift ' of mere wind or anything else invisible. He uses the word of snow (*Progress of Spring*, III.), rain (*Ulysses*), smoke (*Coming of Arthur*), sleet of diamonds (*Vision of Sin*), flickering spectres (*Demeter and Persephone*), and ' drive ' of sunlight (*Rosalind*, III.) and hail (*Sir Galahad*) : cf. LXX. 10. Drifts = winds, is, however, not very far from 'drift-winds' in *The Two Noble Kinsmen*, V. iii. 99, 'waters that drift-winds force to raging.'

15. 'breaks' : cf. *Ode on the Death of the Duke of Wellington*, as quoted on CXXIII.

23. 'Whate'er he be' : cf. CXXIX. and CXXX. 5, and contrast with the frequent speculations on the subject earlier in *In Memoriam*. Perhaps here Tennyson remembered the 'Permitte Divis cetera' of Horace's Ode.

CVIII.

'He will no longer live alone with sorrow, brooding on the past and the mysteries of death and the future life. He will gather from his sorrow some fruit of wisdom for himself and others here on earth.'

5, 'faith' : fidelity (C. E. Benham), but the more obvious sense (faith opp. works) suits the next lines better.

8. 'wells' : see on X. 17.

9-12. The usual interpretation, that the meditations just referred to must be *untrue*, because he simply reads his own thoughts or fancies into the universe, seems to me to disturb the drift of the section. The main point is that these meditations are '*barren*,' 'vacant,' supply no food (4), yield no fruit (13), because they shut him from his kind within the circle of his private grief, and give no wisdom applicable under human skies.

12. 'face' : his own, of course. Cf. *Alastor* :

His eyes beheld
Their own wan light through the reflected lines
Of his thin hair, distinct in the dark depth
Of that still fountain ; as the human heart,
Gazing in dreams over the gloomy grave,
Sees its own treacherous likeness there.

14. 'human skies': in contrast with 7, 8, and in reference also to 1. The poet probably did not notice that 'human' occurs in 12.

15. 'wise': wisdom is one of the 'fruits' of 13. He is now returning to the idea of section 1.

16. Sorrow may bring me wisdom, though not the wisdom you would have brought me if you had lived (that this is the meaning is clear from CXIII.). The line recalls CVII. 23. There, and throughout this section, there is a touch of roughness in the references to the subjects from which he is turning away. The mood is exaggerated, and soon softens. Contrast, for instance, not only CIX. 24, but CXXIII. 9 foll.

SECTIONS CIX.-CXIV.

In his search for wisdom, the 'fruit' of sorrow, he turns to contemplate the character of his friend. The poems of the group attempt to describe this character, a task from which he formerly shrank (see *e.g.* LXXV.). He finds in it the qualities most required to meet the dangers of political and scientific progress, as in the Epilogue he sees in it a type of the humanity of the distant future.

For the connection of this group with the preceding poem through the idea of wisdom, cf. CVIII. 15 with CIX. 24, CXII. 1, CXIII. 1 foll., CXIV. 22 foll.

CIX.

He dwells on the completeness of his friend's character: original, yet critical; logical, yet impassioned in logic; loving good, yet not ascetic;

loving freedom, but an ordered freedom ; uniting the strength of a man with the grace of a woman.

2. 'from household fountains': not 'imported from an intellectual home' (Gatty), nor, I think, defining the talk as about domestic subjects (C. E. Benham), but 'springing from within,' 'original.' Cf. the similar use of οἴκοθεν.

6. Cf. XCV. 29, 30, and XCVI. 13.

13. 'rarely': as in XCI. 2, I presume.

16. Cf. CXXVII. 7 : and, for an exaggerated dramatic expression, the 'Tory member's elder son' in the Conclusion of the *Princess*.

24. Almost repeated in the last line of the Prologue.

CX.

This section refers more specially to the influence exerted on others through social intercourse by the character drawn in CIX.

2. 'younger and elder alike.' 'Rathe' is 'early.'

7. 'the serpent,' accuser and liar.

8. Virgil's 'linguis micat ore trisulcis,' *Geor.* III. 439.
'double': first ed. : 'treble.'

13. 'nearest': first ed. : 'dearest.'

17. 'Nor': first ed. : 'Not.'

CXI.

1 ff. Cf. *The Princess*, IV. :

the clown,
Tho' smock'd, or furr'd and purpled, still the clown.

3. 'To him who grasps': first ed. : 'To who may grasp.'

9. 'act': play a part.

10. 'memories' of mine.

13. 'Best seem'd the thing he was': first ed.: 'So wore his outward best.'

15, 16. Cf. *Guinevere*:

> For manners are not idle, but the fruit
> Of loyal nature, and of noble mind.

18. 'villain': used in reference to 'churl,' the opposite of 'gentle' and 'gentleman' in the technical sense.

20. Cf. LXXXVII. 36-8.

CXII.

The drift of this obscurely written poem appears to be as follows. The poet is criticised by a wise friend because, although he is not dazzled by men of glorious but unevenly developed powers, he thinks little of men of the opposite kind, who have moulded narrower powers into a comparatively perfect whole. But, the poet answers, the reason why a nature of the latter kind appeals little to him is his love for his dead friend, in whose soul new powers constantly sprang into being, and the material fashioned by thought and will was at once so completely fashioned and so vast that it was impossible to hope too much for his future development.

The section is almost invariably misunderstood, because the phrase 'glorious insufficiencies' is (naturally) taken to apply to the poet's friend, and then the poet is supposed to be explaining his admiration for such glorious insufficiency. Yet it is plain (1) that 'gaze with temperate eyes on' does not mean 'admire'; and (2) that the character described in the last two stanzas is not one of insufficiency, however glorious, but one that is neither 'insufficient' nor 'narrow,' but both 'glorious' and 'perfect.' The poet, in short, answers 'high wisdom' by saying: I do not admit that I must choose between glorious insufficiency and narrow perfectness; I reject both, for I knew a man who had the virtues of each and the defects of neither.

2. 'with temperate eyes': the interpretation given above ('undazzled' or 'without much enthusiasm') seems to me the most natural: but it is possible to construe, 'I who tolerate the faults of the great' (C. E. Benham).[1] In neither case can the phrase refer to Hallam.

4. 'set light by': make light of, slight.

8. 'lesser lords of doom': men who, having strong wills, can make the most of the material of their nature, and so control their lot, but who are lesser (than the poet's friend or even the 'glorious insufficiency') because the material is thin. With the phrase cf. 'Men at some time are masters of their fates,' *Julius Cæsar*, I. ii. 139.

13. The material is abundant, *and* it is ordered.

15, 16. Metaphor from tides and moon. Cf. Cowley, *On the death of Mr. William Hervey* (a poem which *In Memoriam* often brings to mind):

> So strong a wit did Nature to him frame,
> As all things but his judgment overcame;
> His judgment like the heavenly moon did show,
> Tempering that mighty sea below.

[1] So also Beeching, 'I who make allowance for the weaknesses of men of genius.'

CXIII.

He imagines his friend entering public life and becoming a great statesman, steadfast in the revolutionary convulsions that may be coming. Cf. LXIV. and Introduction, pp. 6, 8, which also refer to CXIV.

1, 2. See CVIII. 15, 16.

7, 8. He interrupts his question and changes it into an assertion.

14. 'has birth': comes to birth.   With the following lines cf. LXXI. 11, CXXVII., and the poem (in *In Memoriam* metre) *Love thou thy land.*

17. 'thousand': first ed.: 'many.'

CXIV.

He turns from the dangers of the political movement to those of the movement in pursuit of knowledge.   Here too what is most needed he finds in his friend.

The gist of the section is repeated in the Prologue, stanzas 5, 6, 7, where, however, it is said of knowledge, here described as 'earthly,'

And yet we trust it comes from thee [Immortal Love].

For the distinction of knowledge and wisdom Collins compares *Love and Duty*,

The drooping flower of knowledge chang'd to fruit
Of wisdom ;

Locksley Hall ('knowledge comes, but wisdom lingers'); and Cowper's *Task*, VI. 88-99 (where,

O

however, the distinction is not identical with Tennyson's). Cf. *Par. Lost*, VII. 126 ff.

For the division or union of knowledge and reverence (28) cf. Prologue, 25, 26, the *Princess*, VII., and *Love thou thy land*:

> Make knowledge circle with the winds;
> But let her herald, Reverence, fly
> Before her to whatever sky
> Bear seed of men and growth of minds.

For the condemnation of knowledge sought 'for power' (15, 26) cf. the *Princess*, VII., where Ida confesses that she 'sought far less for truth Than power in knowledge.'

4. 'The pillars of Hercules represented the farthest boundary of the ancient mariners' (Beeching).

9. 'vain.' Cf. Prologue, 32 ; *Maud*, I. iv. st. vii.

10. Because she cannot prove a life beyond death : she is 'of things we see.'

12. Allusion to the myth of Pallas springing from the brain of Zeus. Cf. with the condemnation of intellect severed from 'love and faith,' the idea of poetic fancy 'without a conscience or an aim' and so yielding mere 'fantastic beauty' (XXXIV. 5-8).

17. 'A higher hand': that of wisdom (20). The latter word has to Tennyson religious associations ultimately derived from Alexandrian philosophy. Cf. XXXVI. 4, 9.

27. 'by year and hour': first ed. : 'from hour to hour.'

CXV.

'Spring comes once more, and with the beauty of the world his regret also awakes and blossoms.' Cf. XXXVIII. and LXXXIII.

2. 'maze of quick': tangled hedge. For 'quick' cf. LXXXVIII. 2.

3. 'squares': fields. Cf. *The Gardener's Daughter* :

> All the land in flowery squares . . .
> Smelt of the coming summer.

7. Cf. Goethe's *An die Entfernte* :

> Wenn in dem blauen Raum verloren
> Hoch über ihn die Lerche singt.

'living': cf. Milton's 'living sapphires.' The word was a great favourite with Gray and with Shelley, who often uses it of light and colour.

8. 'sightless song': cf. Shelley's lines *To a Skylark*, and Gray's ode on *Vicissitude*, 15, 16 ; for 'sightless,' cf. XCIII. 9.

14. 'greening gleam': out on the sea.

15. 'change their sky': Horace's 'coelum mutant,' *Ep.* I. xi. 27.

18, 20. Cf. LXXXIII. 13-16, and also the budding of the crown of thorns (LXIX.).

CXVI.

'No, not only regret, but life and faith and longing for the friendship to come.'

3. 'the year,' regarded as beginning in spring. Cf. LXXXIII.

5. 'stirring': with the life of insects.

9. Cf. LXX.

11. First ed. :

> The dear, dear voice that I have known
> Will speak.

The original lines seem better than the later version, in which 'once' accentuates the awkwardness of 'have known' used for 'knew.'

CXVII.

' He can think cheerfully of the years that separate him from that friendship, for they will only enhance its delight.' Cf. Shakespeare, Sonnet 56.

2. Cf. LXXXIII. 6.

10. ' steals ': cf. Shakespeare, Sonnet 77, ' thy dial's shady stealth.'

11. ' wheels,' of the clock.

12. Cf. Shakespeare, Sonnet 59, ' five hundred courses of the sun.' Tennyson uses the plural because he refers to the stars as well as our sun. Cf. CV. 25-28.

CXVIII.

This section is connected with CXVII. in so far as it alludes to man's future life, and in so far as both, in a sense, deal with the ' work of Time ' (see line 1 of each section) preparatory to that life. For the date of composition see Introduction, p. 15.

' Do not believe that man's soul is like mere matter, or has been produced, like lower forms in the earlier ages of the earth, only to perish. Believe that he is destined both to advance to something higher on the earth, and also to develope in some higher place elsewhere, if he repeats the process of evolution by subduing the lower within him to the uses of the higher, whether in peaceful growth or through painful struggle.'

Such seems to be the general meaning, but

the section is obscure in parts and it is probably impossible to arrive at certainty as to their bearing. Several thoughts about evolution seem to be in the poet's mind : (1) that there is a radical difference between human love and truth and any earlier product, and that, while the latter arose and perished (as it seems to us) by chance, man is born to develope, both as a race on the earth, and individually in another life ; (2) that nevertheless in this progress the law of the earlier stages still holds good, that the higher must be reached by the subordination of the lower, only now this must take place *within* man ; and that hence (3) his progress depends in some degree on himself (whence the 'if' of line 16 and the imperatives of the last stanza).

1. 'Contemplate': cf. LXXXIV. 1, for the accent.

4. 'as perishable, like the constituents of the body' (strictly, of course, 'like the body of which earth and lime are constituents'). Cf. *Two Voices*:

> Before the little ducts began
> To feed thy bones with lime.

6. 'ampler day': Virgil's 'largior aether,' *Aen.* VI. 640 (Beeching). Cf. Wordsworth, *Laodamia*, 'An ampler ether, a diviner air.'

9. See on LXXXIX. 47 ; and cf. the early *Supposed Confessions of a Second-rate Sensitive Mind*:

> As from the storm
> Of running fires and fluid range
> Of lawless airs, at last stood out
> This excellence and solid form
> Of constant beauty.

10, 11. 'seeming' implies that the appearance of chance and of blind destruction is probably delusive.

12. Cf. LVI. 9. 'Cyclic storms': periodic cataclysms.

13. 'throve,' etc: instead of being the prey of cyclic storms.

14. 'a higher race': the 'great' or 'crowning race' of CIII. 35, Epilogue, 128 ff., and many passages elsewhere, *e.g. The Making of Man* in Tennyson's last volume. In spite of the antithetic 'himself' in 15, the idea is not, I think, of a non-human higher race, as in *Maud*, I. iv. st. vi.

15. 'higher place': than the earth.

16. 'type': represent, be an instance of. Cf. XXXIII. 16 for the substantive. For the verb cf. *Princess*, VII. :

> Dear, but let us type them now
> In our own lives.

There the thing 'typed' is in the future : here it is in the past, so that 'type' almost='repeat.' For this use cf. *On one who affected an effeminate Manner* :

> I prize that soul where man and woman meet,
> Which types all Nature's male and female plan.

The passage beginning with line 16 is very obscure. According to my interpretation two possible ways by which man can repeat the work of time within himself, and so advance on earth and elsewhere, are mentioned ; one is that of steady thriving and adding 'more to more' ; the other that of painful struggle (lines 18 ff.). The word 'so' in 16 would refer to line 13, or 'If so' may be taken together as='if so be that.'

In the first edition, however, line 18 read, not 'Or, crown'd,' but 'And, crown'd': and this (unless 'and' was a mere miswriting or misprint) may indicate that, when Tennyson wrote the passage, he had no such sharp distinction in mind as is implied in the above interpretation, and that 'Or' is equivalent, as several correspondents suggest, to a phrase like 'Or, to put it otherwise.' With this interpretation 'if so' is best taken as = 'if so be that.' But the interpretation does not seem to account for the change of 'And' into 'Or.'

Beeching's note on 'Or,' etc., gives a possible sense : 'To some self-cultivation is possible ; others who are at the mercy of circumstances, may yet transfigure their woes into glories, and forge their character out of calamity.'

C. E. Benham paraphrases : 'if he repeats in his own nature the work of evolution which produced him, or if he so lives combating pain and trouble as to prove that his life is not unwilling to be sublimed.' This is nearer to the text, but surrenders in the last three stanzas the analogy with the 'work of time' which seems to be the main subject of the section.

17. 'from more to more': cf. XLIV. 2.

18. Cf. LXIX.

21. 'central gloom': cf. CXXIV. 23, 24.

24. Cf. XCV. 42.

25-8. Cf. CXX. 11, Epilogue, 133, *The Making of Man, The Dawn, By an Evolutionist, The Ancient Sage* (towards the end).

25. 'use': *e.g.* the use of the 'ends' of 7.

26. 'sensual feast': occurs in Shakespeare, Sonnet 141.

28. 'die': like the 'forms' of 10.

CXIX.

Visiting again the street in which his friend lived, he remembers him happily and 'with scarce a sigh.'

The section forms a beautiful contrast to VII., which is recalled not only by obvious repetitions like those of lines 1 and 12, but by a number of little echoes, such as 'once more,' 'sleeps,' 'street, 'long,' 'early.'

Line 8 points to a late date of composition.

4. Gatty understands a reference to country carts bringing hay, clover, etc., into London. Perhaps the meaning is rather that the silence, the chirping, and the light-blue lane so remind him of the country that he *seems* to 'smell the meadow in the street.' And, again, it is possible, as I am told by a correspondent, that the poet may actually have caught at day-break in London the smell of newly-mown grass wafted from miles away. But I fancy that, if Tennyson had ever had this experience, he would have alluded to it more fully or more than once.

7, 8. 'early': the repetition of the word is, no doubt, intentional.

CXX.

The poem now becomes mainly retrospective. He returns to the thoughts of CXVIII., but also, owing to the intervention of CXIX., recurs to his own 'spiritual strife,' and to the ideas expressed in various parts of the poem regarding the destiny of man (see *e.g.* XXXIV. and LVI.).

3. 'magnetic': cf. CXXV. 15.

4. 1 *Cor.* xv. 32. The mention of 'beasts' in a section which opposes man to 'the greater ape' seems to confuse some readers.

7. Cf. *Vastness*, where he asks what all the sciences are worth if there is nothing beyond death. The idea is not, as some readers suppose at first, that science in proving us to be machines would prove us to be something that could not produce science.

8. Cf. XXXIV. 9 ff. and Epilogue to *Tiresias* :

> What life, so maim'd by night, were worth
> Our living out? Not mine to me.

For an emphatic assertion of Tennyson's to somewhat the same effect see *Nineteenth Century*, Jan. 1893, p. 169.

12. '*born*': first ed. : 'born.' The change was made between 1875 and 1878. But for it the stanza would present no difficulty ; but what is the meaning of the emphasis on 'born'? (1) Is the poet still speaking ironically, and does he mean, 'No doubt, everything is settled for us and nothing by us, and it was settled for me at birth that I should not live like the greater ape'? (2) Or is the emphatic *born* meant to be antithetical to 'springs' in 9? Reference to such passages as CIII. 6 f., Epilogue, 122 ff., *The Coming of Arthur*, *De Profundis*, *Crossing the Bar*, will show that Tennyson thought of birth and what precedes it as, on the one side, a series of physical events, but, on the other side, as the coming of something out of a spiritual 'deep' (cf. Introduction, p. 51, and notes on XLIV. f.). 'Springs' then may be meant to denote the first of these aspects alone, as the only one recognised by materialism ; and '*born*' to emphasise the second : 'the man of the future may consider himself to arise like a mere body, and may act accordingly ; but I for my part am a soul which came from God and will live for ever, and I shall act differently.' Cf. Epilogue, 126, 'be born and think, And act and love' ; and *By an Evolutionist*, 'If my body come from brutes' (but of course the present poem could not possibly refer, as Gatty supposes, to the Darwinian hypothesis, which had not yet appeared, and to which, when it did appear, Tennyson felt no repugnance). (3) Mr. Ferrall suggests that Tennyson means to emphasise the idea that science exists for man, not man for science. 'If future men choose to sacrifice their human *birth-right* to science, let them : I was *born* a man, and will not *make* myself an ape.'

CXXI.

Hesper, the evening star, which follows the setting sun and watches the fading light and ending life of day, is also Phosphor, the morningstar, which precedes the sun and sees the dawn of light and life. They are the same ' planet of Love ' (*Maud*), which does but change its place. And so the poet's past and present are in substance one thing (Love), which has merely changed its place in becoming present instead of past. Cf. CXXVI. 1.

The poem might well have been prompted by the contrast of CXIX. with VII. The idea, as is observed in the *Temple Classics* edition, may have been suggested by the epigram attributed to Plato and translated by Shelley, Ἀστὴρ πρὶν μὲν ἔλαμπες, etc. Cf. *Paradiso*, VIII. 12, and Cary's note.

For the date see Introduction, p. 16.

1. Cf. LXXXIX. 47, 48.

5. 'wain': in some editions 'Wain,' a mere misprint.

9. Cf. IX. 10, 11.

11. 'wakeful bird': cf. *Par. Lost*, III. 38.

12. 'greater light': cf. *Genesis*, i. 16.

18. 'what is one': Love. The next words may be intended to recall, 'I am Alpha and Omega, the first and the last,' *Rev.* i. 11.

19. 'like my present': 'who art like,' etc. Gatty takes the poet's sad present to correspond to the time of Hesper, and his happy youthful past to correspond to the time of Phosphor. But, considering the tone of this part of *In Memoriam*, it seems quite certain that the poet is regarding the past as sad and the present as bright. [It is not, however, *necessary* to suppose that the poet asked himself to which part of his life Hesper answered, and to which Phosphor.]

CXXII.

The poet calls upon the soul of his friend to visit him again.

This section raises perplexing and probably unanswerable questions. (1) The poet refers to some former occasion when his friend appeared to be with him. What is this occasion? (2) In referring to it, he speaks of a time or occasion still earlier ('again,' 'once more'). What is this earlier time?

It is easy and convenient to answer that these two occasions have not been mentioned in the poem: and of course this may be true. But it is surely unlikely that the first of them, at any rate, would be spoken of as it is in this section, unless the reader had heard of it before.

It is conceivable, again, that the reference is not to any particular occasions, but (1) to the unhappy time after Hallam's death, and (2) to the poet's youth before that calamity. But the language in lines 1, 2, 9, 10, 15, seems to convey almost irresistibly the impression that, at any rate, one specific occasion is in the poet's mind; and it seems strange that, immediately after CXXI., the poet should write as if he were less conscious of his friend's presence now than he was in the years of pain. I assume, therefore, that these lines refer to one particular time, and pass to the questions raised.

(1) The obvious answer to the first of them is that the poet refers to the group of sections

XC.-XCV., and particularly to the trance of XCV.
(so Genung and C. E. Benham). For there he
called on his friend to come, and his friend did
seem to be with him, so that the grave did not
divide them; he did 'descend and touch and
enter' (cf. 11 with XCIII. 13); and thereupon the
poet did seem to perceive the agreement of the
motions of the worlds with law (cf. 7, 8 with XCV.
39-43, and 'imagination' in 6 with 'imagination'
in XCIV. 10, and 'thought' in XCV. 38). Cf. also
15, 16 with XCV. 36, 63. But there is a difficulty; for though the first eleven lines of the
present section at once recall the 'trance' of XCV.,
the phrase 'placid awe' (5) seems scarcely appropriate to it, and the last nine lines (in spite of the
resemblances in 15, 16) seem so inappropriate,
and descriptive of an experience so much less
solemn, that one hesitates to identify the trance
of XCV. with the occasion alluded to.

Is there then any other section which can be
taken to deal with that occasion? It seems to me
that the last nine lines recall LXXXVI. almost as
strongly as the first eleven recall XCV. And when
we examine LXXXVI. we find, beside this general
resemblance, some curious similarities of word
and phrase. Cf. e.g. line 11 with LXXXVI. 8,
'fan my brows'; 'fuller' (12) with 'the full
new life'; 'fancy' (17) with 'let the fancy fly';
the collocation of 'gloom' and 'bare the eternal
Heavens' with lines 2-5 of LXXXVI.; the dismissal of thoughts of life and death (16) with the

like dismissal of Doubt and Death in LXXXVI. But again there is a difficulty; for the first eleven lines of this section, though some of the similarities occur in them, seem just as little appropriate to the occasion of LXXXVI. as the last nine do to that of XCV.

Our result, so far, is that the first part of the section recalls XCV., and the second part LXXXVI.; and further that these two parts appear to be somewhat incongruous, an impression which many readers must have received who have never troubled themselves with the point under discussion. Is it possible, then, that the key to this problem lies in the vagueness of the account of the trance in XCV.? The poet himself refers to the difficulty of describing it; perhaps what he felt in it and after it was much more like what he felt on the evening described in LXXXVI. than we at first suppose; and in the same way the experience in LXXXVI. was perhaps more 'mystic' than we at first imagine on reading that poem (which the reader should now re-read in the light of this suggestion).[1] If so, the apparent inappropriateness of the last nine lines of our section to the experience of XCV. is explained; the reminiscences of LXXXVI. are also to some extent explained; and we need not hesitate to hold that CXXII. refers throughout to XCV.

---

[1] So 'Tears, idle tears' was an expression of the *mystic* longings alluded to in *Far, far away* and *The Ancient Sage* (statement to Mr. Knowles); but do most readers understand the poem so?

(2) What then is the time or occasion, prior to the trance of XCV., that is referred to in 'again' and 'once more' (4, 5)? At first sight it is obvious to reply : it is the occasion described in LXXXVI., the poet's feelings on that occasion being *ex hypothesi* not unlike those of the trance ; and here we have the full explanation of the resemblance of parts of CXXII. to LXXXVI.[1] The alternative is to suppose that in 'again' and 'once more' he is thinking of his youth before his friend's death. And on the whole this seems to me the likelier interpretation. It suits the strange phrase, 'like an inconsiderate boy,' and, if the expressions in lines 5-8 seem too strong for a description of a state supposed to be habitual in the poet's youth, we may remember that he was a poet and what he says in *The Poet* :

> He saw thro' life and death, thro' good and ill,
>   He saw thro' his own soul,
> The marvel of the everlasting will,
>   An open scroll,
> Before him lay.

I do not profess to feel much confidence in these speculations, but the reader who thinks them needless will remember that he has still to explain the apparent incongruity of the two parts of the section.

---

[1] One might even go further and suggest that in the second half of CXXII. the poet is actually referring to LXXXVI., the 'former flash of joy' (15) meaning the one that *preceded* the time when he 'rose up against his doom' (2) ; so that the first half of the section would allude to XCV., and the second half to LXXXVI. But I cannot believe this.

[The above is reprinted with a few changes from the first edition, but I feel even less confidence in it than before. I had never doubted, from the time when I first read the section, that it referred to the occasion of XC.-XCV. ; and partly, no doubt, for this reason I could not believe that it refers to no specific occasion. But now that I have become accustomed to the idea mentioned above, and held by Mr. Beeching and Mr. Ferrall, that the poet is speaking of the time of distress and struggle after Hallam's death, and that in 'again' and 'once more' he refers to his youth before Hallam's death, it no longer seems to me, on the whole, unnatural. And it is strongly supported, I think, by the juxtaposition of this section and its predecessor. That says, 'Love was with me in the years of gloom, and is with me now in the revival of joy': this says, 'If you were with me in the years of gloom, be with me now in the revival of joy.'

On the other hand, I still feel the old objections to this view : (a) it does not explain the incongruity between the language of 5-8 and the language of 13-20, which are supposed to describe the experience of one and the same period ; and (b) I cannot bring myself to believe, as it requires, that 'the former flash of joy' means a period of years, even when I remember that this period is perhaps looked back to over ten or fifteen years of sadness. But a suggestion has been made to me, which at any rate goes far to remove these difficulties. (a) In the earlier and later parts of the section the poet

is referring to two distinct *moods* which he knew
in the time before Hallam's death—one mood, a
more intellectual, in which he saw the unclouded
Heavens of law and order; another, in which he
felt the joy of life and sense, and of the play of
fancy. And he says to his friend, 'As you were
with me in my effort to regain the first, so be with
me in the return of the second, and hallow it too.'
(*b*) 'The former flash of joy' is not a description of
the poet's youth; it means, 'the joy that I used to
know in former years,' 'flash of joy' being used
generically. These suggestions give an interpretation of the section which seems to me more
acceptable than that to which I had found myself
driven.

But in reconsidering this matter I have become
more fully satisfied of the truth of the idea that
the experiences described in LXXXVI. and XCV. are
nearer akin than appears at first sight. And in
support of this idea I may call attention to some
further similarities, without discussing their bearing on the interpretation of CXXII. (*a*) Though
the first part of CXXII. reminds one chiefly of XCV.,
and the second chiefly of LXXXVI., yet two of the
striking resemblances already noticed are between
lines in XCV. and in the *second* half of CXXII., and
between lines in LXXXVI. and in the *first* half of
CXXII. Note also (*b*) the meeting of East and
West, common to the final stanzas both of
LXXXVI. and of XCV.; (*c*) the agreement of the
last line of LXXXVI. with the insistence on *peace* in

the last two stanzas of XCIV. (cf. 'placid' in CXXII.) ;
(*d*) the opposition in both passages between this
peace and *doubt* ; (*e*) the idea of escape from, or
victory over, the thought of *death* in LXXXVI. 11 ff.,
XCV. end, and CXXII. 16 ; (*f*) the appearance in
the last line of XCV. of the feeling of triumphant
joy more obviously expressed in LXXXVI. and the
end of CXXII.   None of these resemblances taken
alone would seem significant, but, when they are
taken together and added to those already pointed
out, they become highly significant.   And now
compare with these three sections some lines from
the passage in *The Ancient Sage*, where Tennyson speaks of those appearances in Nature which
especially woke in him the *mystic* feeling (also
expressed in *Far, Far Away*, and *Tears, Idle
Tears*), and brought him 'gleams of more than
mortal things' :

> The first gray streak of earliest summer dawn,
> The last long stripe of waning crimson gloom,
> As if the late and early were but one ;

and compare with the first of these lines the end
of XCV. and also of L. ; with the second LXXXVI.
13, and with that the last stanza of CIII. ; with the
third the similarities noted under (*b*) above, and
the beautiful stanza about the 'first beam' and
'the last' beam in *Tears, Idle Tears*.   Note
finally that this passage in *The Ancient Sage* is
immediately followed by a description of the
'trance' condition, just as in XCV. the 'trance' is
immediately followed by the description of the

P

dawn in which the lights of East and West mingle. The result must surely be a conviction that in many passages where Tennyson speaks of dawn and sunset, with their lights, colours, odours, breezes, winds, setting stars, rising stars (cf. CV. end), we fail to imagine as he imagined, if we do not catch the mystic tone in his voice—that tone which cannot fail to be heard in many of his references to rivers, the deep sea, mountain ranges, where indeed his images often become consciously symbolic.]

1. If the punctuation is right, 'wast thou'='if thou wert' in 9. If a question is intended, there should be a note of interrogation at the end of 8. There is nothing unlikely in the omission of this note (see on LXXXI.), but perhaps the first interpretation is the more probable.

2. 'my doom': of grief. Cf. LXXII. 6.

3. 'yearn'd': first ed. : 'strove.'

4. Cf. III. 6.

13-20. Cf. CXVI. 1-8.

15. 'flash': cf. XCV. 36.

16. 'slip': not 'give free rein to,' but 'dismiss, escape from.'

17. Cf. the opening lines of *Recollections of the Arabian Nights*.

18. He sees prismatic colours in all the dew-drops.

19. The reference may possibly be to the Aurora Borealis, not to an exceptional appearance, heightened by fancy, of lightning in the ordinary sense.

CXXIII.

' The transitoriness of Nature's forms shall not shake his faith in immortality and re-union.'

As in CXVIII. and CXX., he recurs to the thoughts which occupied him when he ' fought with death.' Cf. LVI., and with 4-8 cf. XXXV. 10-12.

This is one of many passages in Tennyson which testify to the great effect upon him of the study of geology. Cf. the fine lines in the *Ode on the Death of the Duke of Wellington* :

> For tho' the Giant Ages heave the hill
> And break the shore, and evermore
> Make and break, and work their will;
> Tho' world on world in myriad myriads roll
> Round us, each with different powers,
> And other forms of life than ours,
> What know we greater than the soul ?

For the date see p. 15.

1-8. G.A.C. compares *Job*, xiv. 11, 18, 19 : " The waters fail from the sea, and the flood decayeth and dryeth up. . . . The mountain falling cometh to nought, and the rock is removed out of his place : the waters wear the stones ; thou washest away the things which grow out of the dust of the earth " : and 2 *Henry IV.* III. i. 45 :

> O God ! that one might read the book of fate,
> And see the revolution of the times
> Make mountains level, and the continent,
> Weary of solid firmness, melt itself
> Into the sea ; and, other times, to see
> The beachy girdle of the Ocean
> Too wide for Neptune's hips !

With which cf. Sonnet 64.

5, 6. ' flow,' ' nothing stands ' : cf. πάντα ῥεῖ, οὐδὲν μένει.

9. ' my spirit ' : which testifies to permanence.

11, 12. Contrast LVII., last stanza.

CXXIV.

In this great poem he still thinks of the spiritual conflict of the past.

'That Nameless to which we call, divined everywhere but not to be understood, where did I find him? Not in evidences drawn. from Nature, nor in questions which the intellect raises and seeks to answer; but when the heart felt and cried upon him like a child I beheld him, and saw that through Nature he moulds man.'

On the ideas used here see Introduction, pp. 54 foll.

2. The context seems to show that the meaning is, 'Present alike in our dearest faith and our ghastliest doubt,' rather than merely, 'Object alike of both.' Cf. XCVI.

3. That Nameless of which we think as one person and as more than one, as the unity in all things and as all things together. Cf. *Akbar's Dream* :

> that Infinite
> Within us, as without, that All-in-all,
> And over all, the never-changing One
> And ever-changing Many.

With 'They' cf. *De Profundis* : 'They said "Let us make man"'; but there 'they' is presumably a reference to the plural in *Gen.* I. 26.

5-8. As the stanza is often misunderstood, it should be observed that the poet does not say that He is not to be found in Nature or in thought, but that it was not there that the poet found Him. *After* He is found elsewhere He is seen also in Nature (see last stanza); and so too 'our little systems' are seen to be 'broken lights of' Him (Prologue) just as Nature 'half conceals and half reveals the Soul within' (v. 3, 4).

14. 'reasons': the reason has been arguing that the world is merely a process of meaningless change (10-12).

16. See p. 62.

17 f. See LIV., LV. I understand the meaning to be : ' No, my heart was like a child crying blindly in doubt and fear. But my blind crying made me wise (*i.e.* I saw that the cry was really, though my heart did not know this, a cry to a father) ; so that I became like a " child that cries," etc.' As Gatty points out, there is perhaps in the phraseology a reminiscence of Herbert's *Collar* :

> But as I raved and grew more fierce and wild
> At every word,
> Methought I heard one calling, 'Child':
> And I replied, 'My Lord.'

18. 'wise': gave me 'wisdom,' though not 'knowledge.'

21. 'am': first ed. : ' seem,' which was in antithesis to ' is ' in 22, and implied that ' I ' is phenomenal.   Cf. CXXXI. 1, 2, and, for ' beheld what is,' XCV. 39.

CXXV.

' Looking back at all his songs, he sees that Love was present in them all, even in the saddest ; and it will abide with him till he goes to meet his friend.'

The poet returns to the idea of CXXI., and in the next section (CXXVI.) he developes it till it almost coincides with one of the main ideas of the Prologue, while others among the following sections lead towards other ideas expressed in that poem. It should be noticed also that the Love spoken of here and in CXXI. is indirectly referred to in CXVIII., CXX., CXXIII., CXXIV., which touch on the conquered doubt whether

> God is love indeed,
> And love Creation's final law.

1. 'said': in conversation with friends (C. E. B.).

2. One naturally takes this to be the principal clause of a sentence; when line 5 will be the principal clause of another sentence. But, if this were so, it seems almost impossible that the second sentence could begin with ' Yea, tho'': and I cannot help thinking that the first five lines form only one sentence, of which line 5 is the principal clause. In that case line 2 may be a parenthesis explaining line 1, or it may possibly be an ungrammatical way of saying, 'Whatever bitter notes my harp might give,' 'which' being understood after 'notes.'

7. Cf. XLVIII. 7-9.

'play'd,' etc.: 'played gracefully with lies.' Perhaps the idea that his friend had forgotten him might be an example.

13, 14. Cf. CIII.

15. 'electric' : cf. CXX. 3.

CXXVI.

' Love is his King. He waits in Love's court on earth, and his friend is elsewhere ; but from end to end of Love's kingdom, which is the universe, pass messages and assurances that all is well.'

1. Cf. CXXV. 12.

3, 4. Cf. Herbert, *Holy Communion* :

While those to spirits refined, at door attend
Despatches from their friend.

10-12. First ed. :

That moves about from place to place,
And whispers to the vast of space
Among the worlds, that all is well.

CXXVII.

' All is well even on earth, though the forms of faith and the social order may perish in the convulsion in which one age ends and another and better begins.'

The first words, and the last lines, of the section link it to its predecessor. ' All is well ' is thus equivalent to ' Love is Lord,' even in the convulsions of human progress, which lead onwards to that ' great race ' of which the poet's friend was a type.

On this section see p. 8, and cf. *Love thou thy land* (written by 1834, *Memoir*, I. 141):

> For all the past of Time reveals
> A bridal dawn of thunder-peals,
> Wherever Thought hath wedded Fact.

> Ev'n now we hear with inward strife
> A motion toiling in the gloom—
> The Spirit of the years to come
> Yearning to mix himself with Life.

> *   *   *   *   *

> If New and Old, disastrous feud,
> Must ever shock, like armed foes,
> And this be true, till Time shall close,
> That Principles are rain'd in blood.

For the date of the section see p. 13.

1. 'faith and form': cf. XXXIII. 3, 4 (where the reference, however, is to religious faith and forms alone). The forms in which faith had embodied herself are deserted by her and become mere 'simulacra' (to use a favourite word of Carlyle, whose writings are recalled by this section). Cf.

The Ancient Sage, 'And cling to Faith beyond the forms of Faith,' etc.

7, 8. Cf. CIX. 16; *Hands All Round* in *Memoir*, I. 346; and the speaker in *Locksley Hall Sixty Years After*:

France had shown a light to all men, preach'd a Gospel, all men's good;
Celtic Demos rose a Demon, shriek'd and slaked the light with blood.

The present lines probably refer to the 'Three glorious Days of July,' 1830, which led to the disappearance of Charles X.

9 ff. 'ill for him': first ed.: 'woe to him.' 'But it is not so with those whose hearts are set merely on temporal glory, or who are spiritually diseased and destitute' (C. E. B.): or perhaps the kings and diseased beggars may be taken to stand for those, at the top and bottom of the social scale, who, from being considered useless to society, are likely to suffer in the period of convulsion here imagined.

With this passage cf. CXIII. 13-20, and a letter on the darkness of the times, 1832 (*Memoir*, I. 99). There are some similar lines in *The Princess*, IV.:

But trim our sails, and let old bygones be,
While down the streams that float us each and all
To the issue, goes, like glittering bergs of ice,
Throne after throne, and molten on the waste
Becomes a cloud: for all things serve their time
Toward that great year of equal mights and rights.

(This 'great year' is of course not the 'great Æon' of 16, but the 'closing cycle' of CV. 28).

11, 12. The 'crags' are, apparently, mountain-tops 'sustaining' spires of ice. Cf. *Prom. Unb.* II. iii.:

And far on high the keen sky-cleaving mountains
From icy spires of sunlike radiance fling
The dawn,

and the application in the lines that follow.

15. 'brute': ponderous: from Horace's *Odes*, I. XXXIV. 9, 'Quo bruta tellus . . . concutitur.' Cf. *Comus*, 797 (Collins).

16. 'great'; first ed.: 'vast.' The change to 'great' was made in the fourth edition, which still read 'vast of space' in CXXVI. 11.

'Æon': cf. XXXV. 11, XCV. 41.

17. 'fires of Hell': the phrase re-appears in *The Princess*, V. 18-20. To recall CXXVI.

CXXVIII.

'His faith in progress on earth is comrade of the love that was undismayed by death (Cf. CXVIII. 14, 15).

The two meet in trust that good shall be the final goal of ill, even of ills that threaten to shake this trust.'

2. 'he': as in XCVII. 2 f.

3. 'lesser,' because man's life on earth offers to faith no obstacle so formidable as death.

5, 6. Cf. *Locksley Hall Sixty Years After*:

Forward then, but still remember how the course of Time will swerve,

Crook and turn upon itself in many a backward streaming curve.

G. A. C. compares Coleridge's *Friend* (*Introduction*, after *Second Landing-place*): 'The progress of the species neither is nor can be like that of a Roman road in a right line. It may be more justly compared to that of a river, which, both in its smaller reaches and larger turnings, is frequently forced back towards its fountains by objects which cannot otherwise be eluded or overcome.' There are other indications that this Introduction influenced Tennyson.

7. 'throned races': races now highest.

8 f. Yet there *is* progress, not a mere repetition of old results that only look like new ; such repetition as is described in 13 ff.

14. 'glorious lies' : Collins quotes the phrase from Crashaw, *To Mistress M. R.* Perhaps Horace's 'splendide mendax' was in the poet's mind.

16. While pretending to produce a new idea.

17. While pretending to abolish it.

18. He narrows himself, but discovers nothing new.

19, 20. Additions which bring no life into what is dead. Bareness' was misprinted 'baseness' in first ed.

23. 'all' : even the eddies of 5 and the degenerations of 7.

24. Cf. *Two Voices* :

> He seems to hear a Heavenly Friend,
> And thro' thick veils to apprehend
> A labour working to an end.

SECTIONS CXXIX. AND CXXX.

His friend has become to him so mingled with all that he loves and worships in the universe that he no longer knows how to imagine him, yet only loves him the more and is the more certain that he can never lose him.

These beautiful poems are almost one ; but the position of the former, just after CXXVII. and CXXVIII., seems to show that the ' dream of good ' in which he mingles all the world with his friend, is a dream of the future of man, while CXXX. refers more specially to the ' mingling ' of the friend with Nature.

Since to the poet Nature and the humanity of

the future reveal Immortal Love, we may compare the two poems with the lines in the Prologue :

> I trust he lives in thee, and there
> I find him worthier to be loved.

But much of the beauty of these sections lies in the expression of an intense affection which has only become deeper as its object has become darklier understood. Cf. Introduction, pp. 47, 48.

CXXIX.

For the structure see note on XIV.

1. 'far off.' This was once the one thing he could not forgive (cf. *e.g.* LXXXII.) ; 'desire': object of desire. Cf. Catullus, II. 5, ' Quum desiderio meo nitenti,' of Lesbia.

3, 4. 'O loved the most,' etc. : and so loved most when felt to be nearest to the highest. Cf. 10 and CXXX. 10-12.

5. 'Known' corresponds to 'human,' 'unknown' to 'divine.' ' Divine': because 'mix'd with God,' or 'living in God' (Epilogue, 140), the 'Immortal Love' (which on its part is human as well as divine, Prologue, 13).

7. 'that canst not die' : like 'hand and lips and eye.'

9. 'Strange': cf. XLI. 5, CXXX. 5. This was prepared for in CVII. 23.

CXXX.

Compare the famous stanzas XLII. and XLIII. of *Adonais*.

1. 'rolling': cf. LXXXVI. 2. Tennyson is very fond of the word.

3. A reminiscence of *Rev.* xix. 17, as developed in *Par. Lost*, III. 621 f. ?

9. Cf. XXXII. 14.

13. Cf. CXXIX. 2.

CXXXI.

The 'living will' invoked in this section is probably interpreted by nearly all readers as the divine will, or the divine love regarded as will. But Gatty's words, 'the Deity,' received the authoritative correction, 'free will in man' (*Key*, 141), and in *Memoir*, I. 319, we read : 'In the same way, "O living will that shalt endure" he explained as that which we know as Free-will, the higher and enduring part of man.' Cf. *De Profundis*, 'this main miracle, that thou art thou, With power on thine own act and on the world,' with Prologue, 15, 'Our wills are ours, we know not how.' Hence this will has to unite itself with the divine will ; Prologue, 16, 'Our wills are ours, to make them thine' ; and hence the divine will is spoken of in line 8 of the present poem as working *with* the human will. For the contrast of this enduring will with 'all that seems,' cf. *The Ancient Sage* :

> But thou be wise in this dream-world of ours,
> Nor take thy dial for thy deity,
> But make the passing shadow serve thy will.

At the same time, it must be remembered that, on the ordinary interpretation of 'living will,' the divine will is regarded in the poem as working in man ; and that the poet's 'Free-will in man' is regarded by him as 'Heaven-descended' (*Will*), and as not only 'apparently an act of self-limitation by the Infinite,' but also 'a revelation by Himself of Himself' (*Memoir*, I. 316).

See also note on line 3. Indeed, it is abundantly evident that in the region of these final poems and of the Prologue 'human' and 'divine' are not regarded as mutually exclusive terms. Cf. *Locksley Hall Sixty Years After*, 'Forward, till you see the highest Human Nature is divine.'

For the structure see note on XIV.

1, 2. The living will 'is,' and therefore endures : cf. on XCV. 39, and CXXIV. 21. 'Will' must not be taken in a narrow sense : the poet did not think, *e.g.*, that 'human love and truth' would not endure (CXVIII. 3).

3. 'spiritual rock' : quotation from I *Cor.* x. 4. Hence the line can hardly mean merely, 'rise in our natures,' but must imply that the will which rises in them springs from a divine source. Cf. 12. Perhaps, as Robinson suggests, there is a reference to *John*, iv. 14, and the phrase 'living water' (cf. 'living' in line 1).

5. 'dust' : the dust of our perishable nature. Cf. Prologue, 9.

7. 'conquer'd years' : cf. LXXXV. 65 f. Contrast I. 13.

10 Cf. Prologue, 4, 21.

11, 12. 'all we loved' lives in 'all we flow from.'

EPILOGUE.

For the occasion and date of this epithalamium see Introduction, pp. 3, 12.

Its purpose is indicated by Tennyson in his remark about *In Memoriam* to Mr. Knowles : 'It begins with a funeral and ends with a marriage—begins with death and ends in promise of a new life—a sort of Divine Comedy, cheerful at

the close.'   But most readers probably feel that
this purpose was already achieved in the final
sections of *In Memoriam*, while parts of the
Epilogue are unfortunately written in Tennyson's
most mannered style.

Miss Chapman gives an excellent summary of
the poem : ' Fitly the Poet closes with a marriage-
song.   For his grief is turned to hope, his weeping into tranquil joy.   Regret is dead, but love
remains, and holy memories, and healthy power
to work for men.   In the union of a beloved
sister with a dear friend, the Poet finds a bright,
harmonious note on which to end his singing.
For such a marriage is the very type of hope and
of all things fair and bright and good, seeming to
bring us nearer to the consummation for which we
pray—that crowning race, that Christ that is
to be.   This perfected manhood towards which
we strive was foreshadowed in him to whom the
Poet sings—that friend who lives and loves in
God for ever.'

1. Cf. LXXXV. 5.

17. See LXXVIII. 18, and CXVI. 9 ff., for the gradual change.

23, 24. The image seems to be that of a brook played on
by sun and shade.   Cf. XLIX. With 'dying songs' (14) cf.
LXXVI., LXXVII. : with the depreciation expressed here the
more serious lines, Prologue, last stanza.

39, 40. Cf. *A Dedication* in the *Enoch Arden* volume.

52. Some particular words must surely be referred to,
but they cannot be any words in the service preceding the
questions and answers of the next stanza.   Possibly Tennyson remembered the Blessing, which follows these questions
and answers and contains the words, 'that ye may so live

together in this life that in the world to come ye may have life everlasting.' But perhaps it is more probable that he refers to the question of the Priest, 'Wilt thou have this man,' etc.

59. Cf. Shakespeare, Sonnet 81, 'Which eyes not yet created shall o'er-read.'

72. Cf. the beautiful passage in the *Excursion*, Book 5, on the graves as seen from the north and from the south.

77-79. 'genial spirits,' 'drooping': cf. *Samson*, 594, 'So much I feel my genial spirits droop.' 'Drooping spirits' occurs also in Browne, *Rel. Med.* I. 32.

'A whiter sun': brighter days: 'white' is used like 'albus': cf. Catullus, VIII. 3, 'Fulsere quondam candidi tibi soles.'

85-8. Contrast XXX. 6-8.

111. 'the shining vapour': see 107.

118. 'tender gloom': cf. Thomson, *Castle of Indolence*, I. lvii. (Collins).

123 f. See on XLV. and CXX. 12.

125. Allusion to the stages in the life of the embryo which appear to represent lower forms of animal life. Cf. perhaps *De Profundis*, 'And every phase of ever-heightening life.'

128. Cf. CIII. 35, CXVIII. 14. 'The crowning race' recurs in *The Princess*, VII.

129. The poet here probably does not mean that the crowning race will understand the mystery of the universe, or be able to prove the truths that can never be proved. The 'knowledge' must be taken in reference to the next lines.

133 f. Cf. CXVIII.

140. Cf. Prologue, 39.

142. 'element,' in which all things move.

143. Cf. LIV. 14, 15, LV. 20, and *The Making of Man* (but in the present passage the poet speaks of the whole creation, not only of the earth).

CHANGES IN THE TEXT OF *IN MEMORIAM.*

I believe the following is a complete list of the differences between the text of the first edition and the text now printed. Most of the changes were made comparatively early : I have added notes on some made later. There seems to have been no alteration since 1884. I note changes of punctuation only where they determine a doubtful meaning. The sections are those of the present text.

	FIRST EDITION.	PRESENT TEXT.
II. 13.	the sullen tree,	thee, sullen tree,
III. 10.	her music	the music
VI. 23, 24.	With wishes, thinking, here to-day,	With wishes, thinking, 'here to-day,'
	Or here to-morrow will he come.	Or 'here to-morrow will he come.'
	[so in 1875]	[so in 1878]
X. 5.	bringest	bring'st
	[change made early, but 'bringest' re-appears in some editions before 1878.]	

	FIRST EDITION.	PRESENT TEXT.
XIII. 13.	me many years	me, many years,
XV. 1.	began	begin
XXI. 25.	And unto one	And one is glad ;
27.	And unto one	And one is sad ;
XXIV. 8.	Since Adam left his garden yet.	Since our first Sun arose and set.
	[so in 1875]	[so in 1878]
10.	Hath stretch'd my forner joy so great?	Makes former gladness loom so great?
XXVI. 13.	So	Then
16.	cloak	shroud
XXXVII. 11.	but	ev'n
19.	as sacramental wine	to me as sacred wine
XXXIX.	[absent]	[added in 1870]
XL. 19.	In such great offices as suit	In those great offices that suit
	[so in 1878]	[so in 1883]
XLIII. 10.	But	So
13.	would	will
LIII. 5.	doctrine	fancy
7.	had not	scarce had
9.	Oh, if	Or, if
	[so in 1878]	[so in 1883]
LIX.	[absent]	[added in 1851, fourth edition]

Q

	FIRST EDITION.	PRESENT TEXT.
LXII. 3.	So	Then
LXVII. 15.	chancel	dark church
LXXI. 6.	So bring an opiate treble-strong,	Then bring an opiate trebly strong,
8.	That thus my pleasure might be whole;	That so my pleasure may be whole;
LXXII. 16.	From hill to hill,	Along the hills,
LXXVIII. 14.	type	mark
LXXXVII. 8.	prophets [so in 1883]	prophet [so in 1884]
LXXXVIII. 6.	dusking	darkening
LXXXIX. 12.	dusky	dusty
XCV. 36.	His [so in 1875]	The [so in 1878]
37.	his [so in 1875]	this [so in 1878]
C. 1.	I wake, I rise:	I climb the hill:
CV. 1.	This holly by the cottage-eave,	To-night ungather'd let us leave
	To night, ungather'd, shall it stand:	This laurel, let this holly stand:
CX. 8.	treble	double
13.	dearest,	nearest,
17.	Not [so in 1875]	Nor [so in 1878]

	FIRST EDITION.	PRESENT TEXT.
CXI. 3.	who may grasp	him who grasps
13.	So wore his outward best,	Best seem'd the thing he was,
CXIII. 17.	many	thousand
CXIV. 27.	from hour to hour	by year and hour
CXVI. 11, 12.	The dear, dear voice that I have known	And that dear voice, I once have known
CXVIII. 18.	Will speak	Still speak
CXX. 12.	And,	Or,
	born	*born*
	[so in 1875]	[so in 1878]
CXXII. 3.	strove	yearn'd
CXXIV. 21.	seem	am
CXXVI. 10.	That	Who
11.	vast	worlds
12.	Among the worlds,	In the deep night,
CXXVII. 9.	woe to	ill for
16.	vast	great
CXXVIII. 19.	baseness	bareness

Q 2

APPENDIX.

PROLOGUE. 5. 'orbs of light and shade': according to the Author's note, 'sun and moon.'

II. 3. The Author's note cites νεκύων ἀμενηνὰ κάρηνα, *Od.* x. 521, etc.

VI. 16. In Crabbe's *Tales of the Hall*, iv., the sea is called the 'moving grave' of the drowned.

XIX. The opening statement in my note is confirmed by Lord Tennyson.

XXV. 1. The Author's note confirms my interpretation.

XXXIII. 8. The Author's note cites Statius, *Silv.* I. iii. 22 :

ceu placidi veritus turbare Vopisci

Pieriosque dies et habentes carmina somnos.

XXXVII. 23. 'the master's field': the Author's note, 'the province of Christianity (see XXXVI.),' makes it probable that 'master' stands for Christ, though it does not make this quite certain, since the 'field' would equally be 'the province of Christianity' if 'master' meant 'the dear one dead' (see 18).

XXXIX. 8-12. The Author's note confirms my interpretation.

XLI. 16. The Author's note, 'the eternal miseries of the Inferno,' confirms, I think, my suggestion that 'forgotten' means 'forgotten by Heaven.' The sufferings are eternal because the judge, after condemning the sinner, never thinks of him again.

XLIII. 10. Prof. Moore Smith has suggested to me that '*garden* of the souls' may be due to recollection of the word Paradise.

XLIV. The Author's note on this much-discussed section confirms my interpretation, súmmarised on p. 135.

As to the metaphor 'the doorways of his head,' it has occurred to me that Tennyson may probably have met with the idea, found in the Upanishads, that the universal soul, or Brahman, enters the body through one of the sutures. The suture is hence called the 'Brahman-orifice,' and again the 'gates of emancipation,' since the soul leaves the body by it at death, and since the body is figured as a house or castle with a number of doors or gates. Thus in the Aitareya Upanishad (*Sacred Books of the East*, vol. i. 241-2) we are told that the soul, or Brahman, after creating the body, meditates as follows (the italics are mine) :

He thought : How can all this be without me ?

And then he thought : By what *way* shall I get there ?

Then, opening the suture of the skull, he got in by that *door*. (See further Deussen, *The Philosophy of the Upanishads*, tr. Geden ; *e.g.* pp. 172, 182 ff., 195, 283-4, 359, 394, 407. The reader will find at p. 283 that the soul at death is said to abandon the body, or rather the gross body, as the mango-fruit leaves its stalk,—a simile which recalls *In Mem.* LXXXII. 7.)

It will be seen that these ideas correspond with the notion, occurring in XLV., XLVII. (see pp. 134, 137), of the general soul individualising itself by connection with the body.

I have not attempted to examine the English books about Indian philosophy that Tennyson might have seen before 1850, but I notice that the passage quoted above is translated by Colebrooke in a paper on the Vedas (1805), reprinted in *Essays on the Religion and Philosophy of the Hindus*, vol. i., 1837. Colebrooke uses the words 'route,' 'way,' not 'door' or 'gate,' but he has a footnote : 'the Hindus believe that the soul . . . enters the body through the sagittal suture.'

I have to thank Mr. M. Hirianna, M.A., who wrote an interesting letter to me from Mysore City on this subject, though, as it happened, after my reading of Deussen's book had led to the above remarks.

XLVI. 15. ' Love, a brooding star': the Author's note, ' as if Lord of the whole life,' confirms the usual interpretation ; but the difficulties of the section remain unresolved.

XLVII. 12-16. The underlying idea is that the souls, whose ultimate nature is light, grow less material and more transparent with each life, and finally melt into *pure* light. Cf. XLI., and ' broken lights' in *Prol.* 19. The rise through life after life is imagined also as the ascent of a mountain, stair after stair. Hence perhaps the use of 'landing-place' for the resting-place at the top. Cf. the use of the word in *The Friend.* I owe these remarks to Prof. A. Carruthers, of the University of Toronto.

XLVIII. 10. My note should be cancelled. Prof. Moore Smith's interpretation seems clearly right ; ' but, by thus sporting with words, the better serves a law of our mental health,' viz. the law not to express sorrow to the utmost.

L. 2. Collins quotes *The Cenci*, IV. i., *sub fin.*:

My blood is running up and down my veins ;

A fearful pleasure makes it prick and tingle.

LV. 11. ' Fifty' should be 'myriad,' says the Author's note (but he did not make this change in the text).

LVII. 10. Prof. Carruthers observes that the effect of ' set ' (sounding at regular intervals) is re-inforced by that of ' drop by drop' in LVIII.

LXI. 9. ' doubtful': I think the interpretation suggested by the passage quoted by Lord Tennyson (shadowy, phantasmal, opp. substantial, true) suits the preceding stanza better than mine ; for in that stanza there is no suggestion of difficulty or uncertainty in discerning the friend on earth.

LXIV. The statement in the first sentence of my note is confirmed, or rather enlarged, by Lord Tennyson's note.

LXVII. 14. ' a lucid veil': the phrase occurs in reference to

St. Kilda, as Wordsworth imagined it, in No. XXXV. of his *Poems composed or suggested during a tour in the summer of 1833*. If this were a case of unconscious reminiscence, LXVII. must be at least as late as 1835, when Wordsworth's volume appeared.

LXVIII. 2. The Author's note refers to *Aen.* vi. 278, not to the place in the *Iliad* to which I referred as the first appearance, known to me, of the idea.

LXIX. My interpretation of the 'crown of thorns' is confirmed by the Author's note.

LXXI. 4. The date of the tour given in Lord Tennyson's note seems to conflict with that given in the *Memoir*, on which I relied. I presume that the latter is correct.

LXXIII. 8. The Author's note refers to Zoroaster's saying, 'Nought errs from law.'

LXXIX. The brother addressed was Charles, says the Author's note.

LXXXI. 1-4. Lord Tennyson believes his father told him that a note of exclamation had been omitted at the end of the stanza. And this agrees with the fact which he mentions, that in a pencil-note on the MS. of *In Memoriam* James Spedding interprets 'Could I have said' as 'I wish I could have said.' Assuming this interpretation to be correct, however, we have still to construe the second stanza. We may either take 'then' in line 5 to mean 'at that time' (so Lord Tennyson), and construe the rest of the stanza as on p. 172 of the Commentary. Or we may take 'then had' to mean 'would in that case have had,' and construe the rest with Mr. Ferrall. I incline to the former alternative.

LXXXVI. 7. 'the horned flood': explained in the Author's note to mean the flood 'between two promontories.'

LXXXVII. 8. It is a curious question why 'prophets' was changed to 'prophet.' Cambridge men seem always to think of King's Chapel in reading the stanza; and Mrs. Verrall tells me that in each of the windows of that chapel there are two prophets, apart from one another and not grouped with other figures. It is conceivable, therefore, that Tennyson, recalling the isolation of the figures, wished to mark it by the use of the singular. But it seems to me more likely that he wished to get rid of a sibilant, or even that the singular was a printer's error which escaped detection.

LXXXVIII. *is* addressed 'to the Nightingale,' says the Author's note.

XCIII. 8. I incline to withdraw the suggestion that the note of interrogation at the end of 4 should be transferred to the end of 8. The third stanza seems to follow more naturally on a positive assertion.

Mrs. Verrall draws my attention to a remarkable resemblance between this passage and the famous lines, *Od.* xi. 601-603 :

> Τὸν δὲ μετ' εἰσενόησα βίην Ἡρακληείην,
> εἴδωλον· αὐτὸς δὲ μετ' ἀθανάτοισι θεοῖσιν
> τέρπεται ἐν θαλίῃς . . .

With the second line of this cf. ' visual shade,' ' he, the Spirit himself,' ' with gods in unconjectured bliss.' These ' gods ' had always seemed to me a little strange. With τέρπεται, etc., cf. XLVII. 9, 10.

12. Lord Tennyson refers ' tenfold ' to the ten heavens of Dante, *Par.* XXVIII.

XCV. As to the allusion to Plotinus on p. 190, see Mrs. Verrall's paper in the *Modern Language Review* for July, 1907, which deals with XCIV. as well as XCV.

XCVI. The Author's note says that the poem refers to Arthur Hallam. Lord Tennyson's note on the last stanza is not intended, I presume, to interpret the last two lines.

XCVIII. My note on the date and occasion of this section (p. 15) was based on a statement in the *Memoir*, i. 148. The Author's note, which says that ' you ' in line 1 is imaginary, contradicts that statement, and, if later than it, may be due to a lapse of memory.

CIII. 55, 56. A note by the Author's wife says that ' the gorgeous sky . . . typifies the glory of the hope in that which is to be.'

CVII. 13. 'drifts': Lord Tennyson agrees with Gatty.

CXII. 2, 3. According to the Author's note, 'glorious insufficiencies' means 'unaccomplished greatness such as Arthur Hallam's.' 'Temperate' must then be taken, with Benham and Beeching, to mean 'calm and indulgent' (Lord Tennyson's phrase).

CXIV. 4. The Author's note refers to Proverbs, ix. 1.

Add, at the end of line 2 of p. 210 of the Commentary : 'also Wordsworth, *Excursion*, iv., the latter part, and *Musings near Aquapendente*, last paragraph : *e.g.* :

O grant the crown

   That Wisdom wears, or take his treacherous staff
   From Knowledge.'

CXVIII. 11. In Lord Tennyson's edition the first word is 'And,' not 'The.' As there is no note, this is perhaps a misprint.

CXX. 9-11. The Author's note runs : 'Spoken ironically against mere materialism, not against evolution.' Perhaps then (I am developing a suggestion of Prof. Moore Smith's) line 12, still ironical, may mean : 'But I must be excused from acting in that fashion, as I happened to be born before materialism was in vogue.'

CXXI. 17. The Author's note runs : 'The evening star is also the morning star, death and sorrow brighten into death and hope.' The second 'death' here seems very strange. If it is right, and if the note truly represents the original idea, my interpretation of the poem, and especially of line 18, must, I presume, be mistaken.

With 17, 18, cf. Ibycus, fr. 42 (Bergk), ὁ δὲ αὐτὸς ἑωσφόρος καὶ ἕσπερος. This astronomical identification, Mrs. Verrall points out, is associated by mystical writers of classical philosophy with the theory of the re-entry of the soul into life after bodily death. It is attributed by Pliny, *Nat. Hist.* II. viii., and Diogenes Laertius, *Vita Pyth.* viii. 14, to Pythagoras. If the Author's note, as it stands, is right, this association may have been in his mind.

CXXIII. 4. The Author's note runs: 'Balloonists say that even in a storm the middle sea is noiseless.'

CXXIV. 18. Lord Tennyson refers 'blind clamour' to 10-12. But, considering the simile of the crying child in 19, and the 'darkness' in 23, I cannot but believe that we have here the image of LIV., referred to in my note, and that the '*blind* clamour' is that of the 'infant crying *in the night.*'

CXXV. 1-5. The following explanation has been suggested to me. The grammatical construction is what it appears to be, 2 being the principal clause of one sentence, and 5 that of another. But, in sense, 3-4 are a heightening of 1-2, and 'tho'' in 3 repeats the 'tho'' implicit in 'whatever.' The meaning will then be: 'Though in all I have said or sung there has been a touch of bitterness; nay, though often there has seemed to be a downright contradiction of hope; yet hope,' etc. This commends itself to me.

CXXVIII. 5, 6. The *Introduction* mentioned in the note was contributed to *The Friend* by Wordsworth.

18. I agree with Profs. Moore Smith and Carruthers that 'cramps' should be taken in the physical sense.

XIX. 7. Mr. John Bailey suggests that 'half' qualifies 'hushes' and not 'the babbling Wye.' This gives a simpler sense to the line, and may be right. Yet the last two stanzas, taken quite strictly, imply that the river is *totally* silent in a part of its course; and LXXXIX. 20, which in form is identical with XIX. 7, also favours in some degree the other interpretation.

XXXIX. I owe to Mr. Robert Bowes the information that this section was first published in 1870, in Strahan and Co.'s Miniature edition of the Works. The date 1872, given on pp. x, 119, 241, has been altered accordingly.

(9)

ENGLISH